THE FEAR OF SUCCESS

THE FEAR OF SUCCESS

Leon Tec, M.D.

READER'S DIGEST PRESS
distributed by
Thomas Y. Crowell Company
New York 1976

 Published simultaneously in Canada by Fitzhenry & Whiteside Limited, Toronto.

Manufactured in the United States of America

Library of Congress Cataloging in Publication Data

Tec, Leon.
The fear of success.

Includes index.
1. Success. 2. Fear. 3. Psychology, Pathological. I. Title.
BF637.S8T3 158'.1 76-14455
ISBN 0-88349-077-3

10 9 8 7 6 5 4 3 2 1

To Nechama, Leora, and Roland,
who were not afraid of my success.

ACKNOWLEDGMENTS

My thanks go to John Tebbel for his invaluable help, to Fredrica S. Friedman for her excellent editorial work, and to Selma Weitz for helpful secretarial assistance.

CONTENTS

Part I

What Is The Fear of Success?

1

DEFINITIONS AND EXPLANATIONS

"Afraid of success? Me? You must be crazy!"

A thirty-six-year-old man made that statement, a statement that speaks for many people today. That man had no obvious neuroses or other disabilities; that man was, in fact, an executive of a large corporation, married and the father of two children. But that man was discontented, uneasy, unhappy—and searching for the reason. In my many years of practice as a psychiatrist, I have come to believe that this restless sense of a lack in our lives, this underlying sense of failure, if you will, is caused not by inability, but by the fear of success.

I believe the fear of success is universal, so widespread that it must be considered normal. It may be severe in some people, less intense in others, but it is always there. Even for those who ostensibly have succeeded and reached the top of their fields, the fear of success may exist and rob them of the enjoyment of their feats.

Obviously, no one *wants* to fail, but most people, unconsciously, do fear success. And thus, in spite of their best intentions, they *do* fail—fail to achieve ambitions, or gain sufficient respect, or make enough money. Some people fail as lovers, others as parents, some even as children. But whatever our situation, it is not unusual for us to feel that we have failed in at least some aspect of life.

The dictionary defines success as "the favorable or prosperous termination of attempts or endeavors," or the attainment of "wealth, position, or honors," or simply, "a successful performance or achievement." In ordinary speech, however, we tend to be more specific. "He's a successful man," we say, implying that he has achieved a prominent position in terms of his wealth or his place in society. Sometimes we're more precise, referring to "a successful mother," or a "successful teacher," or a "successful lawyer." However we mean it, the word implies something necessary in our lives. When we lack the feeling of accomplishment that comes with being successful, life is not very rewarding; life, in fact, becomes a hollow experience.

The fear of success can be defined with equal simplicity. It is an unconscious fear of what one consciously considers important and desirable. To understand the fear of success, it is necessary to consider this variable of our personality in connection with two other adjacent variables, the fear of failure and the wish to succeed. The *fear of failure* may be defined as the *conscious* fear that a person's incompetence will result in specific mistakes. The *wish* to *succeed* may be defined as a person's conscious drive for effective accomplishment of an indicated task. Now the *fear of success* may be seen as the person's *unconscious* fear that his success is not justified and that he is a fraud.

These three variables of our personality are not static

and fixed in their relation to one another, but are in constant flux. They operate in an intertwined and dynamic fashion. When the wish to succeed becomes hypertrophied, for example, it may create so much tension and consume so much energy that unconsciously the person may fear success, although consciously that fear may be experienced as the fear of failure. The dynamics of the success/failure syndrome in the human personality may be seen another way. Every person consciously wants to succeed in the area or areas that he considers important, whether it is money, family, friendship, or career; at the same time, every person consciously wants to avoid failure in those areas. Initially it may appear that the two needs are synonymous and interchangeable. But on closer scrutiny we discover that the wish to succeed is a positive force (provided it is in balance with other components of reality and personality); it is a force of initiative, the power of positive thinking, if you will. The fear of failure, on the other hand, is a negative force; when pronounced, it may be paralyzing and interfere in the attempt to take necessary risks.

Recently a thirty-nine-year-old woman came to see me who personifies the interrelationships of the fear of failure, the wish to succeed, the fear of success. A vice-president and controller of a large company, Ms. F. was about to go to Europe to determine whether her company's French subsidiary should be liquidated. A week before, she had taken a vacation in Aspen, Colorado. She came to see me because of her apprehension. She felt she would fail in her European mission because she had not worked hard during the past few days but had skied and enjoyed herself. Her fear of failure is a conscious one. "If you do not invest full time in your work, you are, well, somehow sinful, and you will be punished—you will fail," Ms. F. said to me. Also consciously Ms. F. wished to succeed, and that is partly why she felt apprehensive about her inadequate preparation for her trip abroad. Her unconscious fear, though, her fear of success, was active and contributing to her anxiety, too. Once I perceived it, it was not difficult to show her how it operated within the dynamics of her personality.

While it is natural for a person who is anxious or upset to look for a recent negative event in his life that triggered his anxiety, in order to discover the fear of success it is necessary to take an opposite position and to encourage the person to talk about the positive things, the successful things that have happened to them. Thus, I first asked Ms. F. what would be the danger if she succeeded in her mission. She was puzzled because she had never considered the fear of success as a factor in her life. But she quickly recognized that there are people in her organization who would resent her success in Europe. She already occupied a position unique for a woman in her company and although lip service is paid to equal opportunity for women, she is painfully aware that the man who is her immediate subordinate and who is two years older than she, with a similar education, thinks that he should have her job. This discussion helped her identify her fear of success. Now that she was free of the unknown source of anxiety that her fear had engendered, she was able to determine that more than ever she wished to do a good job, employee resentments notwithstanding. With that resolution, she was able to take care of the work that would enhance her effectiveness on her European mission.

The fear of success is a *fear* precisely because it threatens the individual—it endangers him psychologically. So long as that fear is not conscious, it packs even more psychological power; one cannot do anything about something one does not know. Once recognized or acknowledged, though, the fear can be neutralized through rational analysis and behavior. The important difference between the fear of success and the fear of failure, as we have noted, is that the former is usually not recognized. People have never come to me with a complaint about the fear of success, but they recognize it when I point it out. They grasp the negative aspects of it first: functions unfulfilled, promotions prevented, talent inhibited, family life complicated, parent-child rapport spoiled. Only after initial recognition of the effects of the fear of success do its positive aspects emerge because such knowledge stimulates thought, introspection, and energy for action. Usually people say, "I won't let this fear dominate my life any longer. I'm going to do something about it."

A case in point is Mrs. S., a woman in her forties, the mother of four children, who had a hectic time with her husband's drinking problem. One day we were discussing her college dating experience and she told me that she used to avoid boys whom she thought she could wrap around her finger. Mrs. S. believed it was wrong for anyone to dominate another human being. If she helped her husband to remain sober, if she influenced him, it would mean she manipulated and dominated him, and that was immoral, she said. I offered her two alternatives. She could leave her husband to inevitable destruction and death (he had already suffered three coronaries) or she could accept the "omnipotent" role of trying to change him. Confronting these choices, she saw that she no longer could refuse the obvious and she decided to try to shed her fear of that particular success. When Mrs. S. dared to take a position on her husband's drinking, he determined to help himself and he has not touched alcohol for two years.

As we have already seen, the fear of success surfaces at different times in different people's lives. In some people the fear of success appears early in life and is triggered by some minor incidents. I remember an adolescent who came to see me. He was troubled by the anxiety he felt every time he ventured from familiar territory. We learned that as a toddler his mother responded to his frequent peregrinations with vehement "no's." Unconsciously he had bridged his childhood and adolescence with the same fear. Adults, of course, continue to do the same thing. How many of your friends are afraid to fly?

In some other people the fear of success surfaces only from the impact of heavy burdens or dramatic circumstances. A successful architect came to see me maintaining he was having a nervous breakdown. First we discussed his work, then his family situation. It turned out that the dramatic circumstance that had precipitated his fear of success had occurred when his daughter was chosen to lead the debutante ball. "Why is that bad?" I inquired. "She might be injured, attacked, even raped with that public exposure," he said. Unconsciously, though, it turned out that this man feared he might succeed in seducing his daughter, whom he had kissed and fondled as a child and whom he now, for the first time, perceived as a woman.

There are those persons who fear additional success and future achievement, while others fear the success they have already achieved. A lawyer who had just graduated from law school, where she had been editor in chief of the law review, and also worked part-time to support herself, walked into my office. Hired by a major law firm as an associate, she questioned her ability to function. Actually, though, she felt frantic because her past identity, that of a struggling student, was no longer operative. Now all of a sudden she was a financially solvent adult and she had not yet recognized it.

In spite of their accomplishments, there are also people who fear success because they have a poor image of themselves—an image they do not like. They may have had fathers who neglected them, and they fear they will repeat that negative example. Consider the persons who look at their "successful" fathers and observe that they seldom smiled, that they seldom seemed happy. Why, then, they ask, should they emulate or continue to emulate that life-style?

When I discuss the problem of successful people who unconsciously fear success, a fuller picture of the fear-of-success syndrome begins to emerge. Here is a man who fears that a series of successes must lead to ultimate failure, and another who believes that staying in the background guarantees safety, or at least will not reveal his frailties, shortcomings, and general weaknesses. Doubt and fear spring up in these people the first time they ask themselves, "What price success? What will it cost me? What will it do to me? Is my family going to suffer? Will I be corrupted?" They seek help from a therapist not because they understand that the fear of success has brought them to that point of despair, but because their lives have become too painful to carry on alone. The fear of success becomes visible only in the course of discussing other matters.

Actually, there are two distinct aspects to the fear of success. One is what the outsider sees—that is, people who are not in the individual's inner circle. A college professor, for example, may seem very successful in the eyes of the public and his students, but not to his peers. The insiders may have a different, critical view for several reasons: They know more about the field, they are envious, and they are near. Proximity as well as familiarity breeds contempt. The college professor may be appreciated by outsiders and even by his peers, but he still may have great doubts about himself. All his achievements and honors may seem to him a mistake. He fears that one day the world will discover the truth about him—that he is an intellectual imposter—and therefore the more successful he becomes and the higher he goes, the harder he fears he will fall.

The same principle applies in business. The board chairman of a billion-dollar corporation came into my office because his insecurities spoiled his achievements for him. He was perplexed because he knew that people in his corporation saw him as highly competent—"The buck stops with me," he said—but he did not feel sufficiently competent. He was aware that many people wanted to be in his position, just as he had before he reached it. But thirty years ago, when he started in business as a young college graduate, he thought of that position as a pleasant daydream, not as a reality. For many years there was always a boss above him. Reaching the top, he had a reaction to being there. The reaction was a dizzy spell, so to speak, an emotional vertigo. His self-image had not caught up with his professional skills.

This case also illustrates the second aspect of the fear of success—not how the world views the man, but how the man sees himself. A man knows that an advance results not merely in a new and larger office, a different relationship with employees and other business associates, a different perspective, but in change, and that gradually, insidiously, his life will be different, and whether he likes it or not, so will he.

We can see this effect in another way, in the case of the college senior who is upset when he gets a scholarship from the graduate school of his choice and is also appointed a teaching assistant. "I would rather be number two than number one," he tells me. "I don't want to have to prove my worthiness. I'm lazy and I don't want responsibility, but I like recognition." To him the danger of being prominent is equated with the danger of responsibility, which he fears.

There is another variety of this particular fear of success that I call the "number-one man and number-two man game." The first succeeds and worries, the other makes sure never to reach the pinnacle. He may do many things correctly, but he will also get one or two things wrong. I have been assured by a wide range of such people—businessmen, athletes, scholars—that they would rather be number two than number one. "If I only made a greater effort," they say, "I could easily be number one." But when I have talked to them, to their great surprise they discover that they have a fear of winning and that they can't sustain the effort required to do better unless they learn how to get rid of that fear.

Intensity is a prime factor in this game. Success may exercise a very positive influence on our lives at a moderate level of intensity, but it may be destructive at a higher level. If a person doesn't evaluate his investment in psychic time and energy properly, success can be devastating because it goes beyond the optimum of his emotional endurance. This happened recently to a full-scholarship student at Princeton who had ranked number two in his major department for his first three years and then moved into the number one position in his senior year. He soon developed intense anxieties that caused him to drop out of college. He just could not accept the fact that he no longer had anyone to top.

Sometimes the fear of success is so intense that it cannot be modified, even with the help of long-term psychotherapy. Then there is a need to lower the person's ambitions or to agree that for him less achievement is more functional. We have to remember that there is a large discrepancy between intellectual development and emotional readiness to meet the challenges of life.

One of my earliest patients taught me that. Mr. O., at our first meeting, told me he was going to pieces. I learned that shortly after he graduated from college, he had become a psychologist for the personnel department of a large corporation. Soon he was getting regular increases in pay and then he was put in charge of personnel counseling. This new responsibility weighed heavily on him. "I have to send out dozens of letters every day. How can I be sure the right piece of paper is in each envelope?" he said, panic in his voice.

I could see he was desperate. I advised him to take a leave of absence from his job. During this time he underwent additional therapy and seemed to recover his self-confidence. Then he was able to resume his work. However, he was again so good at his job that his employers told him they were going to make him manager of the entire personnel department. That did it. Mr. O. called me in a panic, asking my advice, and I told him to try it. I thought that the success would be good for him. But now I believe I was wrong and that he may have been right in what he did next: He quit his job and became a janitor and groundskeeper for a preparatory school at one-fourth his former salary; later he called to tell me that he was happy. Mr. O. had feared the kind of success that he might have gained with his talents and settled for a success that was less threatening to him and that was therefore more real.

Physically, the fear of success, even when it is psychologically unconscious, may be accompanied by disassociated sensations of nervousness, including stomach flutters, erratic heartbeat, sweating, jerky or semiparalyzed muscles. It is a great equalizer, this fear. It may be a vice-presidency a man hopes (and fears) to get, but in his dreams about it he may have all the terrible sensations he would experience if someone were trying to throw him from the top of a skyscraper. Again, it may be an unpleasant childhood we want to forget, but the fear we suffer in seeking independence can be a fear of hunger, of thirst, or of banishment. And yet again, it may be a lover we desire, and desire to please, but we may be completely crippled in the process by anxiety symptoms that are the result of deep-seated inhibitions from the past.

In short, it's fair to assert that the fear of success is the fear of being mortal. When I say this, I realize that this explanation is a departure from the orthodox. I am not now defining success in one of its dictionary senses as "the favorable termination of a venture." Life is a venture, but nevertheless its termination is death, and that can be favorable only if living seems unendurable. Before death can be accepted it must be preceded by fulfillment of life, a satisfaction that comes from an ongoing experience. We want to feel that we have done what we could, been good at what we were fitted to do, enjoyed self-respect, felt free to move constantly from one full moment to the next, and, in Kipling's phrase, enjoyed the privilege of filling each "unforgiving minute with sixty seconds of distance run." That, I believe, is success. I follow this premise with another. In his evolution, man has made a virtue of fearlessness. Thus the fear of success is inimical to the human condition and for this reason alone must be resolved.

To illustrate further how the fear of success operates and how it may be recognized, let me offer myself as another case history. When I entered medical school at Vilno, Poland, in 1937, I often played poker in the evenings with some of my fellow medical students. Since we were serious students, the games were short, usually from 10:00 P.M. to midnight. The stakes were small; it was rare for anyone to win or lose more than ten *zloty*, two dollars in those days, or about a week's spending money.

One night I had an extraordinary winning streak. My cards were good, but even when they were bad I somehow dominated the three other boys. Again and again I bluffed and was not called. By eleven o'clock I had about fifty *zloty* in front of me; the others were down to nothing and borrowed from me. "You can't go home early tonight," one of the boys said, "not with a bundle like that."

A few hands later, after I had won still more, I had a strange feeling. I was suddenly disinterested in winning and morbidly sure I was about to lose. I wanted the money I had won, but knew with certainty that I was going to give it back. That was exactly what occurred, and by midnight I had lost even a few *zloty* of my own. After the game I attributed this turn of fortune to a combination of bad luck and compassion. I told myself that the other students were even poorer than I. Knowing what I know today, however, I realize that I suffered that night from the fear of success. My self-image was not that of a winner at cards and I have learned that, when one's self-image does not match one's accomplishment, the fear of success dominates.

Not long after I graduated from medical school, I contracted a severe case of paratyphoid fever and spent two months in a hospital. I was in a ward with twenty-four other patients, running a fever nearly the whole time and suffering discomfort and general malaise. There were others worse off. Across from me a young man lay dying from ulcerative colitis. Next to my bed an older patient was in serious condition after a massive coronary attack. Next to him was a man with a bleeding ulcer. In spite of the prevailing misery and agony, we contrived to tell jokes and to pass the time as pleasantly as possible.

Then I improved and was told that I could leave. Shortly thereafter I went to a convalescent home, where the food was good and the care excellent. Nevertheless, I was amazed to discover that now I was depressed, dejected, and in fact had lost most of my interest in staying alive. I moved like a robot. Conversations did not intrigue me, and I found myself irritated by other people. I felt the only thing I wanted was to return to the hospital. I resisted the idea, but it was extremely difficult. Reflecting on that episode, I now understand that at that time I was also suffering from a fear of success—specifically a fear of recovery and the attendant responsibilities.

Once I understood the gambling and the hospital episodes, I could recall other examples of the fear of success in my earlier life. I remembered a fight with a cousin when I was eleven. He was older and larger and consequently won easily when we wrestled. But one day I was angry and suddenly found myself so strong that I had him down on his belly securely scissored, with his arm bent painfully across his back. If I forced it up another inch, he would beg for mercy, but I could not give it that final push. I knew that I did not want him to surrender. Instead, I let him up and we called it a draw.

At thirteen I found myself torn emotionally by a larger success. It was 1932, Poland lived under the benevolent dictator, General Josef Pilsudski, and at our school every child was asked to write an essay about his accomplishments. I abandoned the conventional chronological approach the other students were employing and used the flashback technique to tell Pilsudski's story. My essay won the district prize. The district commander, a general close to Pilsudski, came to my hometown one evening to hear me read the essay to the assembled town officials. I could face that audience without a tremor, but I knew that I could not face this success and the response it would evoke within the framework of my own family. I told my mother and father that I did not want them to attend my triumph. They asked me why and at that time I didn't know the answer. All I knew was that I was painfully anxious at the thought of their being there. Now I know it was because I would be, even temporarily, more important than my hero, my father, and that was a conflicted self-image for me.

Father took this strange request calmly because he was preoccupied with his apothecary's business, but my mother could not stand the thought of losing this moment of maternal pride. After telling me she would not come to the hall, she stood outside in the darkness, watching me through a window as I read my essay. Now that I understand this incident, I realize there was nothing unusual in my behavior. It was typical of a child's fear of success.

Then the war came and after it ended I went to New York, where I achieved a lifelong ambition by getting a posdoctoral residency in psychiatry at Bellevue Hospital. One night in 1953, as the resident on duty, I was called to the emergency room to take care of a man who had turned himself in to a policeman with a cry for help: "I'm going to commit suicide, Officer. Please take me to the hospital." I found the patient waiting for me, sitting in one of the cubicles, his head in his hands. He was a mild-looking man, about thirty-five years old, and I was astonished when he identified himself—he was a well-known writer of humorous pieces and I had often chuckled over his work in magazines.

My job was to admit him, confirm the diagnosis of "suicidal depressive," and write out the necessary orders so that the nurses could give him sedation. While I was carrying out this routine, I was still puzzling over finding such a prominent man in the Bellevue emergency ward. Curious, I talked to him for more than half an hour, and as we talked, the reason for his trouble gradually emerged. He told me he was depressed because one of the magazines that he had been free-lancing for had offered him a permanent staff job. He needed the money and security the job represented, but he was convinced he was not competent to handle it, and if he took it, he would soon be exposed as a fraud. There was no apparent rational cause for that fear. He was a successful writer whose work was regarded as nothing less than masterful.

But then he told me what was at the root of his fear. He felt himself to be a fraud because he could not sit in an office and write his stories on a typewriter. He had to write with a pencil, his feet higher than his head, a drink by his side, and he could not face the thought of having his behavior exposed. In an office, in the company of cool professionals, he was afraid he would not be strong enough or brazen enough to carry on his accustomed creative rituals.

I thought his fears were exaggerated. I told him that the organization that had made him the job offer was large enough to respect and accommodate his creative habits, and this appeared to reassure him. Ten days later he was released and, in an optimistic frame of mind, took the job.

Although he never became a regular patient, I followed his career with more than ordinary interest. In his new position he had complete freedom and privacy, so that for a decade, his fears apparently gone, he wrote prolifically and well. Then a new editor took over and reorganized the physical facilities of the magazine so that this writer now had to share an office. At that point the fear of success, which had been dormant, intensified to such a point that it became a wish for failure in every part of his life. He divorced his wife, he even broke up with his mistress, and his drinking increased from heavy indulgence to alcoholic compulsiveness. He no longer wrote well enough for publication. After several years of this degeneration he reached the point once more where I had first discovered him. This time he succeeded, with an overdose of sleeping pills. The fear of success finally had brought him to the suicide he had confronted years before.

Suicide, of course, is the extreme manifestation of the fear of success. Marilyn Monroe's life, for example, was a narrative of self-destruction, and whether she meant to die when she took barbiturates while she was drinking is immaterial. If her performance ability had been supported by self-appreciation and a basic trust, she could have thrived on her status rather than have been destroyed by it. Ernest Hemingway, another noted suicide, and the son of a suicide, was never satisfied with the literary achievements that had brought him fame, nor with the nonliterary pursuits that had brought him satisfaction earlier. In the end he lived with a compulsion to write better, hunt better, fish better, and make love better. In his case success could not be recognized and therefore it could not be experienced.

Through my work I have learned that the fear of success takes many forms. For a child it is fear of growing up, and the fear of not growing up when we're adolescent. For a lover, it is fear of abandonment and consummation. For a young parent, it is fear of self-effacement and replacement. For any patient, it is the fear of being cured—the fear of rounding a corner ahead and turning into an unknown street, the fear of completion and fulfillment. The fear of success occurs regardless of color, religion, gender, or age. It varies in intensity and surfaces in various forms, but it is part of every person's experience, male or female. Today we are recognizing, though, that for women there are special problems: They may not fear only successful competition with men, but also a more subtle competition with other women.

"I would rather let Jane get Michael," Ms. K. said, "because she went with him first, and anyway I'm not good enough for him." By means of this self-effacement, Ms. K. camouflaged her fear of intimate relationships.

Research has shown that in the area of successful competition with men, women in medical school associate the wish to be at the top of the class with thoughts of depression, illness, and even death; by contrast, men are taught to connect success with happiness and prosperity.

For another example, twenty-year-old Ms. M. was at the top of her class from the first grade on, until she fell in love with a twenty-four-year-old high-school dropout. In a short time her marks in school dropped sharply, she was failing three subjects and had two incompletes. When we talked about her situation, it was clear that her fear of academic success was connected with a vague suspicion that her boyfriend would frown on her academic achievement.

In women, fear of success also may be connected with a fear of change, even when it is a change for the better. I knew an eighteen-year-old girl whose father used to get violently angry with her, kick her, slap her, and lock her in a closet. This girl became worried when therapy changed her father and he began to treat her with respect. She feared that "he might not be the same" if he improved too much. No matter how much she resented his violent ways, she didn't want to lose the father she knew. The new and more relaxed man who was emerging might become unrecognizable as the entity she called "my father."

Men, too, suffer from the fear of change. I was anxious about undertaking the task of writing this book. I asked myself how much of my anxiety was the fear of failure and how much the fear of success. Before I was aware of the latter, I would have accepted the former, but today I know better. In attempting to answer my own question I found myself struggling with conflicting forces. There was the wish to express my thoughts, to share with a large number of people what I consider useful and even essential knowledge. But I was conscious, too, of the criticism I could expect to get from those who disagreed with me. And suppose the book was well received and turned out to be extremely popular? Could that be

because it might propel me into a more
ht create new and unfamiliar situations
tive of anxiety.
we have the conflict of the adjacent forces
lity: the fear of failure, the wish to suc-
f success. Together they contribute to the
ess. I have been able to deal with my fear
use I understand it. I believe anyone can
ear of success who will learn to identify it.
nd confronting the fear of success without
tionalization is the primary step in dealing
with it.

Part II

Growing Up Afraid of Success

2

IN THE BEGINNING

The Peter Pan Syndrome

In my private practice and as director of the Mid-Fairfield Child Guidance Center in Connecticut, a psychiatric clinic for patients from toddlerhood to adolescence, I have noted one inescapable fact: many of us learn to renounce success while we are still young. We're small children then, so small that "elves can reach up to whisper in our ears," as the poet Francis Thompson said. Pygmies in a world of giants, we are easily frightened, easily impressed by our own helplessness and dependence.

Announcing some early fears of success, those childhood attempts to modify reality, Marsha, four, says: "No, I don't like dolls. They wet their pants." And five-year-old Horace declares, "I'd like to kill Dad, but I'm too little." And John, age seven, his face darkening under his freckles, sums it all up: "I'm never going to grow up. Not as long as I live."

These articulations illustrate a fundamental of childhood that I call the Peter Pan complex, a testimonial to the cry of recognition and identification that greets Peter's defiant "I won't grow up!" This fear of growing up is probably the most conspicuous form that the fear of success ever takes, especially in childhood, and it originates because a young child is unable to understand that he will grow to be big, strong, knowledgeable, and competent like his parents. Consequently he soon reaches the conclusion that he is an inferior being—or, in the language of transactional analysis, "You're OK, I'm not OK."

Nine-year-old Jean still felt that way. Originally from France and in the United States for only two years, he came into my office a victim of his classmates' cruelty: They teased him unmercifully about his foreign accent. At the end of our first session Jean said, "I like the way you speak, Dr. Tec, and I hate the way I speak." And I speak with a Russian accent!

No matter how well an individual eventually overcomes his initial fear of success, vestiges of his early self-image remain in everyone's consciousness for life. Most of us make do with this legacy, some more successfully than others. But a few of us become addicts of failure. On the basis of my professional experience, I have worked out several practical suggestions on raising children and dealing with their fears of success that I think can be helpful.

Heredity and Conception

The first suggestion I have is so simple as to seem fatuous. When I express it, people often look at me with disbelief. Nevertheless, I must say it: Have healthy babies. Everything that parents or psychiatrists can give a child in later years, good or bad, is less significant than the genetic program conferred on him at the moment he is conceived. Unfortunately, we know relatively little about that moment. There are few experimental studies on the factors that might help determine the roll of genetic dice in conception. It seems incredible that our sophisticated scientific society has neglected this aspect of reproduction, but it is so—almost as if our scientific culture itself feared success and virtually ignored a question basic to its survival. We do know, however, that nature has fixed the wheel of genetic fortune so that the odds are heavily in favor of evolution and species improvement. The sturdiest sperm swims the fastest and fertilizes the ripest egg in the womb. Still, the conclusion to be drawn is obvious: In both mother and father the best health of mind and body will give nature, evolution, and the eventual child the best chance.

In line with this information, it is wrong for parents to believe, as they often do in these times especially, that the nurture they give their children can be blamed for everything that goes wrong with them. Nothing is farther from the truth. Because of his genetic makeup and body chemistry, every child creates his own environment. Brothers who are treated alike may turn out to be as different as Cain and Abel. A child can be born restless, hypersensitive, or clumsy as surely as he can be born with blue eyes, a cleft palate, or a high I.Q. He can be genetically predisposed to alcoholism and schizophrenia, or to congeniality and exuberance.

This does not mean that parents should abdicate their traditional function—parents still have a most important role. They can complicate inborn peculiarities, making a child feel like a misfit, or conversely, they can help a child take pride in himself. Their love and support, or their lack of love and support, will determine the child's initial sense of self, and of the world as a hostile and threatening place or as a positive one.

And that brings me to my second point: In the human experience, development is not a fixed thing but a fluid entity. This means that genetic predispositions, first behavioral patterns, even early traces of the fear of success, are subject to constant modification within our twelve-billion-cell computer brain. In replaying experiences, in regressing to childhood as we do frequently when we remember early incidents from our lives, the brain edits the lessons stored in our memory banks. And while we can never entirely change our first impressions of life, we can adjust them by subsequent replayings, strengthening or weakening them, or relegating them to the bottom of buried piles of information in the most dusty and inaccessible corners of our minds.

A friend of mine is a professor at a leading university. Yet in her childhood she was considered a poor student and less gifted than her sister. She accepted that role for years, until through serendipity she found a special interest that propelled her into her success. Ever since, she has been examining and reordering her initial impressions of herself to conform to her new image. That's the normal, healthy task of psychological life that most of us perform periodically at every stage of our lives. It is just that critical procedure which allows us to improve our legacy.

Womb World

From the moment a child is conceived, he begins interacting with the outside world of chemical, neurophysiological, and social experiences. The consistency and quality of those messages are important to the child, for the fear of success may emerge from cumulative inconsistent and inadequate messages. Some of these messages precede birth, some follow after, yet even these can be reversed or eliminated through better understanding.

In the uterus, a child is dependent on his mother's heart and lungs for sustenance through the umbilical cord. If the mother is healthy, the regular thump of her heart and heave of her lungs provide the child with a comforting rhythm. When a pregnant woman suffers from cardiac arhythmia (asthmatic gasping) or from the hacking cough of a heavy smoker, the unborn child must learn to tolerate a syncopated rhythm out of step with his own autonomous body processes. These offbeats, provided they are not too erratic, may be stimulating for the healthy and adaptive child. Sometimes, however, they disrupt a child's development and in later life result in a high incidence of nervousness and insecurity. Thus, at this early stage, a child may acquire his first, preverbal fear of success. He "expects," for instance, a surge of oxygen-rich blood, and doesn't get it. The embryonic brain compensates and makes allowance for the possibility that gratification will not always follow preparation for it, and this psychic allowance creates a climate of anxiety within the child, or at least a potential for anxiety.

Life in the womb ends in what may be another fear-inducing experience in the child's existence: passing down the uterine canal and out into the world. There are psychiatrists who place a great deal of emphasis on birth trauma and attribute any number of effects on later psychic development to it. The chief merit of this notion, in my view, is that it can never be proved. The memory of birth trauma, if in fact it exists, lies too deep in the preverbal mind ever to be probed.

Newborn babies certainly don't look as though they have been traumatized as they sleep peacefully or lie wakefully alert in hospital nurseries. That is particularly true of those whose mothers did not have an anesthetic. Most children, then, are built to withstand the birth process and benefit from it—it wakes them up to life; it is their first success. For some, though, the ordeal is an experience that implants fear, expressing itself later in recurrent anxiety in situations of stress, and negativism about pushing through to successful resolutions of problems. Such anxiety and negativism, if not dispelled by less difficult successes in subsequent experience, can fuel the fear of success in general.

A Friendly Eye

Life in the womb is warm, well regulated, and blind. Outside it can be chilly, hectic, and ill regulated for unfortunate infants, but for all of them it is no longer blind. That is the big difference after the fetal experience: The child literally has seen "the light of day," because human eyes open at birth. Thus the infant is able to see threats long before he is capable of protecting himself from danger.

The human optic apparatus is also a prime input for programing the brain. Other animals hear and communicate by sounds. Human infants hear and communicate with their mothers through tones of voice, but they cannot learn language until they are well along in seeing, in recognizing faces and facial expressions, and in coordinating hand, mouth, and eye. Infants who see without yet being able to *do,* search about for a pair of friendly eyes, finding them usually in the mother's face. After birth the ability to find a friendly eye, to find security and well-being, may become a prime mechanism for avoiding the fear of success at that stage of life.

As we have noted, fear of success builds on fears left over from the past. The two most important are the fear of height and the fear of eyes—that is, fear of falling to death and the fear of being seen and slain. Babies' first games, specifically drop-the-rattle and peek-a-boo, are most significant in light of these fears.

Dropping the rattle and then flinging it away as soon as it is given back is a counterphobic game. It teaches the infant to grasp and release an object—a basic form of advantageous behavior, and at the same time the baby gains reassurance that fallen objects are not necessarily destroyed. It is thus a therapeutic game to help overcome the vestigial fear of heights and falling.

As for the game of peek-a-boo, it has always been believed, and correctly, that the baby finds it reassuring because it makes mother's face reappear at will after a brief disappearance. By playing it, the baby learns to cope with his anxieties about separation from his mother and gains confidence that out-of-sight people or objects are not lost forever. But there is another reason that makes peek-a-boo a universal game of infants, and that has to do with the more inherent human cause for the fear of success than the fear of heights and falling—the fear of eyes.

We can learn about this fear by comparing its mechanism in animals and humans. Experiments have shown that feigned death and its temporary paralysis in animals is triggered by a fear of being noticed—a fear of eyes. A beast has to be seen before it can be captured. Wild creatures track each other by smell and hearing, but the attack is made only when the prey is in sight. "Playing possum," a state of suppressed life signs, appears to be almost entirely a response to the glare of eyes. In the laboratory a test rabbit will go into deep shock, playing dead, if it sees the eyes of the assistant holding it down. This instinctive passive response to discovery by a hostile eye goes back at least to the age of reptiles, a hundred million years ago. That is why the double aces on dice, the symbol of immediate defeat, are called "snake eyes." And similarly, the mythology of the "evil eye" is found in nearly every language and culture, to imply a paralysis induced by a hostile, threatening force.

While in animal life such a sight response may be a matter of life and death, in human society this fear is rarely so realistic. By and large there is no danger in being looked at, but still the fear of eyes persists. Freud had a shrewd appreciation of mankind's fear of notice, and consequently of prominence and success, long before our present clinical knowledge confirmed it. He had no corroborative evidence, but he put down his ideas in a short, relatively obscure essay entitled "Those Wrecked by Success." In it he described the personality disintegration suffered by some of his patients at the very moment of their achievement and public prominence.

I recently had a case that exemplifies Freud's point. A young teacher, age thirty-two, was promoted to assistant principal of his school. A bit apprehensive, he was nevertheless managing, when the principal had a heart attack. After only two months as assistant principal, my patient was appointed principal. Immediately he could not function. He suffered from severe headaches, depression, and the inability to make a decision or to complete his work. "Everyone is always looking for me, looking to me, staring at me now in school," he said. "I can't stand it."

No doubt if Freud had been able to perform the appropriate experiments, he would have stressed the importance of being looked at in subsequent psychic development. It is reasonable to suppose this because he candidly acknowledged that he suffered uneasiness when he had to face staring eyes. That was one of the reasons he made his patients lie on a couch, where they would have to look at the ceiling.

In my own practice, however, I feel that a person deserves to be encouraged to look into the doctor's eyes and I avoid the couch as much as possible. I believe that the instinctive fear of success, or the fear of being noticed, must be treated by showing that the fear is exaggerated. I counsel eye contact and "playing alive," because shrinking from notice and playing possum are not advantageous to human behavior. When I discussed these views with the young principal he soon could recognize their validity and return to work, his fear of success in check. Thus I would suggest to parents that they practice such steady and focused interaction with their children from the start. A direct and friendly eye can go a long way to dispel the fear of success.

Big Mouth

As soon as the umbilical cord has been cut, a child's will to live is centered in his mouth. By means of an intricate genetic program, the mouth is a pathway not only to the stomach but to the brain as well. Purposeful sucking, then, is a necessary stage in a child's neurological development. The rubber nipple has been available for little more than a century, but the nipple of the breast has served as a stimulus and response since the evolution of the first mammal. Consequently, in my view, it scarcely makes sense to substitute one inventor's artifact for a biological system developed over a period of 70 million years, and I recommend breast-feeding whenever possible. I do this because it is important for a child to consummate his sucking urges. The infant learns to enjoy success by striving for it and having to suck hard. Given a breast, the infant will always get a little milk for his efforts, and since rewards achieved through effort are the most memorable, he is not likely to forget his mother's love.

On the other hand, if he gets all the sucking he wants on full bottles, he may easily imbibe to the point of indigestion. When the child is sometimes given a full bottle and a flow-through nipple, and at other times an empty nipple-pacifier, he experiences extremes of hunger gratification and hunger frustration, of rewarded sucking, and of sucking for its own sake. The two artifacts, bottle and pacifier, and the two processes, feeding and sucking, become separated in a way that would never happen from the gradual exhaustion through sucking of the milk supply in the mother's breast.

Regretfully, a mother who decides to nurse her child may have to overcome opposition from professional medical personnel. Things are changing, of course, but in many hospitals the staff would still rather not break routine by having to pick up a crying baby and carry him to his mother. The aide in the nursery prefers to give the infant a bottle herself.

Recently a young woman told me about the ordeal she went through in order to nurse her own baby. She had inverted nipples, and when the obstetrician looked at her, he declared, "You won't make a good cow."

"I have no intention of becoming a cow," she told him.

"You're a pretty girl," the doctor said, in a way that

would have driven a feminist up the wall. "Why not leave well enough alone?"

The young woman told her husband that she might have trouble nursing, and that if she didn't have a chance to work it out during the first few days in the hospital, the milk would dry up. They both decided to talk to the nurses in advance. "Even so," this woman told me, her voice still full of fury, "you have no idea the ways they can find to sabotage you in a hospital. My first three feedings were a disappointment and I was in tears—no one would help. Then that night, late, I was finally lucky. A really smart nurses' aide brought my baby to me and sat by and encouraged me. She knew a thing or two, that girl. She showed me how to pop out the nipples and keep them popped out by relaxing. I've had no problem with nursing since then, except I sometimes still get mad when I think about what a hard time I had at first with no support in the hospital."

A baby deserves success in feeding, surrounded by his mother's warmth and attention, and while I personally feel that the intimacy that comes from breast-feeding is superior, I do recognize that many women prefer the other option. As long as the food comes with personal warmth and affection, it will provide the child with the most important aspect of nurturing.

Crawling Columbus

To be successful, a human being must enjoy taking small, calculated risks and venturing occasionally into the unknown. A child first learns to forage afield and return in triumph when he is crawling. Each of his small excursions can be a lesson in either success or in the fear of it, depending on the mother's attitude. A good mother begins to apply at this point what is probably the most important single rule of family raising: Whenever possible, let a child determine his own distance from you.

This is good advice in dealing with dependents of any age. Trying to be close to a standoffish teenager, for example, almost always has the opposite effect. Of course, not even the most gifted individuals ever achieve a sense of secure freedom in everything they undertake, but most of us could accomplish more if we had been given a better taste of freedom while we were still within reach of mother's apronstrings.

Room to roam is particularly important to a toddler because he is just forming his attitude toward adventure, an attitude that will affect the creativity of his entire life. Thus he should be given enough hazard-free space to discover himself. Ideally, a child ought to be able to use his mother as a base camp for explorations in all directions. Then the child would go as far as he wanted, handling and mouthing what he could, periodically returning to his mother for reassurance and recharging his emotional batteries.

The mother should try to see that her child's explorations bring him some gratification without serious harm, but she shouldn't go overboard to protect him. If she always could manage to keep the child from bumping his head, an impossibility, she would also keep him from ever learning how a banged head feels. Further, the mother who swoops down regularly, with palpable alarm and fear, punishes the explorer emotionally for his adventure, and the child inevitably records in his brain: "unpleasant—frightening—avoid." This imprint creates a specific fear of physical success and is in sharp contrast to the simple "avoid if possible" impression left by casual intervention.

On the other hand, if a child constantly bumps his head and his mother turns a cold "I told you so" shoulder, that can be more damaging. Such a child might well go through life figuratively banging his head and screaming for someone to pay attention. The sensible mother avoids both these extremes, giving her child enough tether to find minor misadventures and enough love to solace the small hurts that inevitably follow.

A visible flaw in a child compels a mother to think through the responsibilities of motherhood, but if no flaw meets the eye, the mother may create one by an undisciplined use of the child as an extension of herself. If she suffers acutely from any fears in herself, especially fears of physical pain, she may implant these, too. In effect, she says: "Johnny, be careful! You have to remember you can't do that! I did it once and it really hurts." Mary's case illustrates this maternal effect as it evidences itself in the post-toddler.

Mary was brought to see me because she was afraid of going to school. Living in a big house on five acres, she had not been able to have many unsupervised encounters with children her own age. During her preschool years her family had moved several times, and now new moves always gave her "butterflies in the stomach." Having spent two nights in a hospital with a broken leg when she was two, she also said she didn't like such institutions. To her, school had the same kind of impersonality.

For a seven-year-old, Mary was an extraordinarily composed, articulate little girl. We talked over her school fears while playing some games and painting some pictures; during this time I found that her muscle control and powers of concentration were both well developed. Then we went out into the yard, where she used the swing and the trampoline with a grace and abandon that told me she was a natural athlete. She wouldn't climb a tree, however, because, as she explained coolly, that was how she had broken her leg when she was two. So we went back into my office and talked some more.

"I can see why I shouldn't be afraid," she said, "but I still don't want to go to school. It's such an ocean."

I was mystified by that reply. Later I talked at length to both Mary's mother and father. The mother was a fragile, nervous, urban kind of woman. The father was more like his daughter—a natural athlete, easygoing, open. To pursue the clue I had that didn't fit, the fear of the ocean Mary had expressed, I talked further with her mother.

"Oh yes, I'm positively terrified of the ocean," she told me. "I think I must have had a favorite fish or something that drowned in daddy's aquarium tank. I never went to the beach much as a child and I never did learn how to swim."

"Do you ever go to the beach now with Mary?" I asked.

"We used to. As a matter of fact it's my fault she's afraid of the water. Do you think that's important? During the summers when she was a toddler, I used to take her to the beach club. I lay there sunning and she dug sand. One day I rolled over and saw her out in the water swimming. She was just a little girl and I thought she couldn't possibly swim. So I rushed out into the water and rescued her."

Mary's mother had snatched her from the water at the moment she had precociously succeeded in teaching herself how to swim. The mother had been equally anxious about Mary's first day in school, and the little girl, associating the two anxieties, equated a fear of the water with a fear of school. That fear intensified her normal school shock and made it unbearable.

Often the mother's fear is so intense that the child camouflages it with a taboo about some related object. A clear example of this psychological extension was the case of five-year-old Mike.

Mike's family lived on the tenth floor of a high-rise apartment building, and he made his mother walk up and down all ten flights every time she took him out to school, or for a walk in the park, or a visit to the supermarket. The reason for Mike's fear wasn't clear until, having gained his trust, I had a meeting with him and his mother to discuss the problem. Early in the session he went to the heart of the matter in the blunt manner of children.

"But, Mom!" he cried out, "you're afraid of escalators."

Then the story came out. In a department store one day, Mike's mother, in terror, had plucked him back from a down escalator. Other children had been playing on it, walking up it and spanking their hands against the moving rubber handrails. Mike had wanted to join them, but his mother suffered from a phobia about down escalators, although she wasn't afraid of those going up.

Leading Mike away, she took the elevator, and while they were riding down in it, she scolded the boy severely. He was so frightened and frustrated by this episode that he had felt as though the world were collapsing and smothering him. In the elevator of the apartment house where he lived, he felt for the first time the terror of his new fear, and from that day on, he "punished" his mother by making her walk up the stairs.

Most small children can make a healthy adjustment to maternal panics and personal fears, but as in Mike's case, to be successful the process sometimes requires displacing the urgent emotional part of the mother's warning to other objects. For the most part, then, parents at this stage are at their best if they are simply there when they are needed, caring but not interfering, conversing but not converting, towers of watchfulness, compass points of known coordinates, and centers of personal activity who teach by example rather than by oratory.

Saying Yes Instead of No

From eighteen months to three years, a child begins to realize that he is a separate and distinct organism from the world around him. This conclusion is reached in a manner not entirely unconscious. In fact, it is often at this point that a child's growing vocabulary reflects his awareness of his new identity: "Want" becomes "I want"; "give" becomes "give me." This period of separation and individuation is also a period of negativism: The mother says "no" and the child adopts it as his own powerful statement.

Beneath the surface, however, the child is regrouping his forces for new conquests, coordinating himself, learning to run instead of stagger, and to pick up as well as clutch. "No" simply repeats the chief emphatic that he has heard until that time. He is not indicting his parents or society at large, but trying to draw back and figure out the laws of the world in which he lives. Some "no's," he finds, are conditional and depend on the situation. Others represent universal laws that seem to apply, however, only to children. A few are categorical and apply to the giant adults as well.

The negativism that is healthy in the toddler learning to identify with the power of the adult who uses the word "no" to him may persist unhealthily into adulthood. Then it would become a fear of success in relating to other people. I remember a banker whose early childhood was dominated by two powerful, negativistic people: a forbidding mother and a forbidding older sister. Even as an adult he clung unwittingly to his negativism, going so far as to begin every sentence with a "No." "No, I don't want to go the opera. No, I won't see that client. No, don't interrupt me now." He was obviously threatening and disagreeable to people, but for him cordial interpersonal relations would be too much of a change from his familiar family pattern.

In the normal child, while he is learning a new language and digesting the knowledge that he is an individual organism, he is also forming his first conscious relationships with others. He sees that these other individuals may be friends or foes, in or out of harmony with himself and with each other. Usually he is forced to confront the competition of brothers or sisters or neighborhood children. He sees conflict between fellow children and within the giant retinue of his adult servants. Mother disagrees with father, or with grandmother, or with aunt. The child is still only learning language, but he quickly correlates the words he hears with the tensions that accompany them.

The years from one and a half to three are strewn with submerged rocks on which a child may build a fear of success. Thus the child needs to be talked to and talked in front of, for everything is grist to his mill. If talk and storytelling are combined with holding and fondling, a positive earlier association, the child will acquire the gift of tongues even better. Too much verbal praise for a child's inborn learning skills, however, can impede his progress toward achievement and also impart fears of success. Children overreact to the demands made on them, both negatively and positively, and they are the most sensitive to these demands when they are learning language and trying to absorb what their parents tell them.

If a child's mother is too relieved to see him talking instead of prowling, she will tell him, in effect, that talk is better than action. This, obviously, is the fear of success that has impaired many capable intellects, including Aesop's fox, Hamlet, and Walter Mitty. Too much negative emphasis on language can have a similar effect. I know a talented author whose mother was always encouraging him to go out and play. Even before he was three, she would not permit him to play quiet games of exploration or examination in the house, but sent him out into the "fresh air." He was a gifted intellectual, but an awkward athlete. Yet to "go out and play" became an obsession with him. He broke bones and acquired scars in sports at which he was never proficient. As an adult he impaired his health on exploratory trips to Brazil, New Guinea, and Africa, and he frightened himself while proving that he could parachute and sky-dive. His mother made him an outdoorsman, but she couldn't suppress his gift for words. In spite of himself, he read books and eventually wrote them. He was nearly fifty, however, before he could believe that his profession as a writer was honorable and that he needn't risk his life in physical pursuits that would please his mother.

In attempting to twist children from novelists into athletes or dancers into account executives, parents are simply passing on their own hangups, overapplying and overinterpreting codes of ethics and childcare they learned as children. But the child may develop a fear of success. An example is the boy who wants to be a pianist, but whose parents want him to be a mathematician. If he pursues his musical career and becomes a success, he proves his parents wrong. But defying their wishes and sacrificing their emotional support may be too much for him, and he may succumb to his fear of success so as not to prove his parents wrong and so as not to threaten their love for him.

Other parents, for another example, react with outraged morality to their children's tall stories and bragging. Yet bragging has a place in the home, not only for the child but for the parents as well. Home should be a place where everyone understands and makes allowances, where no one has to keep his guard up all the time. In public, of course, bragging can be extremely offensive, but when social conventions against it are brought into the home and applied too rigidly, it may lead to hypocrisy or pent-up rebellion, especially in the teenage years.

Fourteen-year-old Burt's parents had brought him to me because of his ritualistic compulsions. The confrontation that occurred in my office was abrasive and revealing.

Burt opened the session by telling me an old joke. I laughed politely, and Burt's father said, "Don't try to make it look like a social visit, Burt."

"Don't be so uptight, Pop," Burt said. "A little joke can't hurt."

"You're stalling, Burt," his mother interposed.

"So what's to talk about?" Burt said defiantly. "Just get off my back, that's all."

"Always the tough big shot," his father said.

"Yeah, I used to be conceited, but now I'm perfect," Burt said.

"Okay, let's talk about your rituals at home," his father snapped back. And suddenly Burt looked chastened.

"Rituals?" I asked.

"Yes, he locks his door and pulls the blinds on the window and lights black candles."

"I have to clean up the wax, so I know what color the candles are," Burt's mother added.

"Nobody's allowed in," Burt's father said. "The whole ceremony is top secret."

From Burt's silence and obvious embarrassment, I judged that the black rites he celebrated were probably involved with sexual fantasies of some kind and were the accompaniment to masturbation practices, not at all uncommon among adolescent boys.

"Tell me . . ." I began.

"It doesn't seem normal to me," the father interrupted.

"It frightens me," his wife chimed in.

Burt lifted his head and offered a defense of sorts: "I got first honors in school."

"So what's that got to do with it?" his father said. "You're bragging again to divert attention."

"You want the whole world to know your honors," the mother said, "but you can't tell your family your dishonors."

I finally got a word in. "There's a difference between the family and the whole world," I said.

"Is that an excuse for starting to brag all the time?" Burt's father demanded.

"It is if he couldn't brag when he was younger," I said.

"But always wanting to be the center of attention?" the mother demanded.

"Only in the family," I said. "Inside the family should be a friendly resting place."

"You see?" Burt exulted. "I do good at school, so why can't I say what I want at home?"

"Is it catching up on baby bragging to burn black candles in your room with the door locked?" his mother asked.

I laughed, but Burt interrupted, his voice icy and intense. "Dad never brags," he said. "He's so modest he blushes every time he gets into his Lincoln Continental."

"That's unfair, Burt," his mother said. "It's a comfortable car."

"Well, how about your diamond choker?" Burt said. "Doesn't that choke you up so you don't need to brag out loud?"

"We worked hard," the father said.

"So do I," Burt yelled, "and that's why I brag, but no one pays any attention."

To tell a child that bragging is wicked usually does little more than increase his deviousness and guilt. The same point may be made about lying. Children generally lie to escape punishment or embarrassment. Sometimes they lie to spare the feelings of others, peers or siblings, and sometimes they lie for fun, simply to test the gullibility of their parents. Often, in the best tradition of television, they lie to sell their parents on an outing or an acquisition. When parents are not deceived—and that is most of the time since children's lies are generally so transparent—it's best not to accuse the prevaricator of wrongdoing. Parents need to empathize with a child's need, without condoning the bad action. For the young child often brags and lies as extensions of his creative imagination. The adult who had unnecessary restrictions on his creative thinking—as a child he was always told to support his assertion with facts—may suffer from a specific fear of successful speculative thought. If he uses his imagination, he will defy his parents and create an unbearable conflict. To avoid such conflict, that adult may deny creative thought and the result may be a sterile life.

Most lies fall into two categories: guilty and unnecessary. In my experience, parents constantly tell their children unnecessary lies, such as "You're not going to get shot," on the way to an inoculation. In spite of this semantic evasion, the child is furious. Tommy, age five, knew he had to have a tonsillectomy, that he was in for something unpleasant, and that he would suffer a little, but on the way to the hospital his mother assured him that he was only going to see a big balloon full of gas. The balloon wasn't the shape he had expected, and it was full of ether. When he awoke with an intolerably sore throat and his first hangover, he blamed his mother severely for her unnecessary lie. "You lied to me, you lied to me, it hurt!"

The fear of truth is socially a major fear of success, spreading from individual to individual and entrapping whole nations. Ours is a society of traditional deceit in many respects, but it is also a society of credit. Our science and technology are based on honest experiments and truthful expositions of evidence. Consequently, a child needs to be impressed with the utilitarian advantages of honesty.

Most of the frauds and false representations for which society metes out harsh punishment have their origin in family attitudes toward childhood bragging. The child needs to be able to magnify his heroisms in order to gain a positive self-image. Often he exaggerates his feats outrageously simply to gain an ear. Mothers who do not listen to their children's tall stories will be told taller and taller ones.

The best mother listens to all her child's stories and gives positive approval to those that are appealing. At the same time she suggests indirectly that boasts and fantasies are best understood at home. Such encouragement and understanding are part of the process by which children are guided out of the no-saying period to the stage where they learn to say yes. A good example of how this transition can take place is the case of two-year-old Chub.

When Chub was brought to me by his parents, who were worried because he frequently refused to eat, sometimes for two or three consecutive meals, I put a family of dolls on my office floor for him to play with. He spent the first minute or two huddled on his mother's lap, but then he climbed down and headed for the toy furniture and the dolls.

He put the baby doll on the toy sofa and then screamed at it, "No, no, no!" Chub's mother was about to intervene, but I held up my hand and we watched.

Chub had the father doll spank the baby doll. "Real hard," he shouted. "You bad boy!" The father started up from his chair, but I waved him back.

Chub next staged a fight between the mother doll and the father doll.

"Mess!" yelled the father doll.

"Go 'way!" screamed the mother doll.

"Hit you!" yelled the father.

Chub sent all the dolls flying across the floor. Then, without a word, he put the baby doll on the father doll's shoulders, stood the father on a toy chair, and deliberately knocked the chair over. Then he did the same thing with the mother doll and the baby doll. After that he rose to his feet with satisfaction and carried the toy bed over to me, as though to put it on my desk. That was too much for his father.

"No, Chub," he said. "No, don't touch the doctor's desk."

Chub's mother was halfway out of her chair as I said, "It's all right. He can play on my desk."

We watched while Chub arranged a dining room of toy furniture opposite me. Every time he put down a piece, he shouted, "No!" and then moved the piece slightly. Finally he sat the father doll on the highchair and placed the mother doll beside it.

"Throw up!" he commanded. He reached for one of my pencils and struck down both the parent dolls. With that his mother leaped to her feet, grabbed the pencil from Chub's hand, and said, "No, darling, that's Doctor Tec's pencil."

Later I had a session alone with Chub. His play with the family dolls again consisted of forbidding the baby to do something and punishing it. But again the baby took over and rode on top of the parent dolls, and finally the baby fed the parents and they both threw up.

After that, I coached Chub's parents in a variety of ways to say both "yes" and "no" effectively to help mute Chub's negativism, and I insisted they allow the boy not to eat whenever he refused. In a matter of weeks, conflict gone, he was eating sturdily, and affirmation in the household was increasing rapidly.

I had a follow-up session with Chub shortly before his third birthday. He played with the baby doll, the older brother doll, and the older sister doll. He arranged and rearranged the toy furniture for the doll's house and kept saying, "Yes" and "Oh boy!" The sister got scolded when she kicked her brother, but not a single "no" was said to the baby doll. I offered a piece of candy to Chub, which he would have reached for eight months earlier even while saying, "No!" Now he took it gladly and said, "Thanks."

Having learned to talk, having tried bragging, storytelling, and even lying, children next go on to a new mountain-climbing stage in which they begin to test their powers of speech, listening, and learning. At few other turning points in life do they feel more creative and more ready for success. At just this point, however, they encounter the stumbling block of gender, of knowing themselves as boy or girl, and wondering about the mystery of sex.

3

THE CHILDHOOD STEEPLECHASE

Presumptuous Sex

I once had a woman patient who fled from her own reflection. She couldn't comb her hair in front of a mirror, and she hated window-shopping because she would see herself reflected in the glass. Her face was scarred with exacerbated acne, largely self-induced because she was constantly clawing and picking at her face. This woman saw herself as neither girl nor boy; in fact, she feared to see herself at all.

Not many of us are afraid to look into the mirror, but almost everyone has some doubts about the self-image we see with our inner eye. A good self-image and the attendant courage about success have their best chance of developing during the early years of childhood. Positive infantile experiences of the kind I've described are obvious prerequisites for successful life. A child has to be secure about eating and being loved before he can grow. He has to dare to use his arms and legs before he can learn to move successfully, and he has to learn to talk before he can think logically.

All these elements—pride in eating, moving, and talking—begin to come together at about the age of three and lead to a sense of gender identity. At about three, too, the child starts experimenting with calculated affirmations. He begins to answer "yes" to questions, and to talk of having "friends." How much fear of success and poor self-image have already crept in can be gauged by the speed and certainty of the move from "no" to "yes."

Even nervous, fearful children get a tremendous boost from their attempts to talk positively. Three-year-olds are typically exuberant, confident, energetic, cheeky, trying on all sorts of new acts. They begin to play games of make-believe with others and embellish the stories they tell. At the same time, they begin consciously to explore their own bodies and the bodies of their playmates.

If the child's realization that he is sexually distinguished by either a penis or a vagina comes as an interesting but dispassionate discovery, it is usually because the youngster has been allowed to make this discovery for himself, without obtrusive parental commentaries. In most families, however, children are immediately taught a set of attitudes toward their genitals. Moralists say this is the place to begin teaching right and wrong. Feminists charge that this is where prescribed role-playing begins. Most psychologists see this stage as an opportunity to direct the development of sexuality as a learning experience and to prevent patterns of guilt and fear. Many parents, however, find themselves unable to cope with the child's discovery of his genitals, especially when that discovery is accompanied by shame, even though they may have induced that feeling from the beginning, consciously or unconsciously.

Common attitudes are reflected in the case of the mother who came to me because her seven-year-old was having erections and he was disturbed by them. She recounted the incidents that had led her to seek my help.

The trouble began when the boy came to her and complained, "Ma, my thing is sticking out again."

She felt herself grow pale, sweaty, and awkward, although she did not think of herself as a prude. "That's not so bad," she managed to say.

"Do something about it," he demanded. "I don't want it. I wish I could cut it off."

"It's not so bad," she repeated.

"But it's sticking out," he shouted. "I can't go to school."

"It's all right," she said. "It'll go away."

Of course, it did, but the boy did not go to school and the scene was repeated a few weeks later. After a half dozen more recurrences, the mother was desperate. I advised her to change her tone. Next time her son came to her with an erection, I said, she should simply smile and continue her work. At first the boy wasn't satisfied with her new calm and lack of interest, but little by little, over a period of several months, he came to her with erections less and less frequently.

Today, far fewer mothers are saying, "Don't play with yourself!" as they did a generation ago, but most still cannot fail to react to what their child is doing. It turns a mother on or turns her off, and the child will not fail to notice the sudden rush of conversation with which she tries to divert him and herself. To try to ignore what he is doing seems little better than to condemn it, she thinks, but most mothers find it difficult to give quiet approval, thus missing an excellent opportunity to teach the child the difference between private and public behavior.

"What you're doing is all right," the knowledgeable mother will say, "but it's something you do in private in your own room. It's like urinating, and the rule is not to do it in front of anyone except yourself."

Girls are less likely to be observed masturbating by their parents. They are usually more sensitive to family feelings and practice their discovery secretly. Those who don't, however, should be given the same direction toward privacy.

Some therapists think that parents should learn to talk to their children about sex, difficult as it may be for many of them. Excellent books are available on the subject, and the rewards for the effort are great, not only in terms of freer and easier relationships within the family but also in doing as much as parents can to provide the foundation for a healthy, happy, adult sex life.

One of the objectives of sex education should be to put sex in perspective, to treat it as healthy and natural, an important part of everyone's life that should not have an overwhelming relationship to all the other parts. A sex therapist who specializes in these matters has written that the most important sex organ we have is between the ears, and it is how we feel and think about our sexual behavior that matters. Listening to children talk about sex, listening to the questions they specifically ask, is better than talking to them or at them, in my opinion.

One of the problems parents confront when their children reach three is their wish to marry the parent of the opposite sex, about which so much has been written since Freud first translated it from literary into psychoanalytic terms. This drama is one in which the child not only senses a physical bond between the parents, but directs his burgeoning sexual interest toward the parent of the opposite sex, thus creating a rivalry with father or mother. The classic unresolved Oedipus complex, in which boys feel they have to compete with their fathers for the mother's love, or the Electra complex, in which girls compete with their mothers for their father, are staples in literature and have been factors in the sex lives of millions of people. But it need be no more traumatic than any of the other crises of childhood if it is handled intelligently.

I once told an obstreperous three-year-old named Billy: "You can't marry your mother."

"Gee, what a shame," he said. "She's such a gorgeous girl."

Sometimes parents find the "family romance" frightening and even take it seriously. They don't understand that a four-year-old boy doesn't literally want to marry his mother and get rid of his father. Not only does he not know what "sleeping with" entails, but he feels pride in his father and needs him. His desire to marry his mother is only the first expression of his masculinity. When he is told that this is impractical, he usually passes on to other concerns. The problems come only for the child without a clear sexual identity—is he a boy or a girl?—for then he cannot resolve the natural sexual conflict with his parents at this stage. Those persons who cannot move on to the next step of interpersonal relationships wind up as emotional isolates. We all know those persons who wish to spend their free time alone; we also know those persons in the midst of social gatherings or even family who are alone despite the fact that they are surrounded by people. When a child has a fear of success about his sexual identity it obviously creates difficulties in several areas, as the next case illustrates.

Rod looked manly enough when he sat down in my office, but his mother told me that in a fight with his elder brother he had scratched like a girl, and on the school bus he had been seen kissing another boy.

"I wanted to get him away so I could have both seats to myself," Rod offered in his own defense.

"But he doesn't fight back at school," his mother said. "He lets the other boys beat him up."

"That's not true!" Rod said.

"Well, the teacher told me that either you scratch and kick like a girl, or you let them beat you up."

"What would you want to be if you were born again, a boy or a girl?" I interposed.

"Both."

"Both boy and girl? Is that possible?"

"No. I want to be a tomboy."

"A tomboy is a girl who behaves like a boy."

"Yes, that's what I want to be."

"Really?"

"Sure. Girls are luckier than boys. They go first in everything. For a spelling bee at our school the teacher picked two girls instead of a boy and a girl."

Eventually, after several years of therapy, Rod was able to accept himself as a boy. It happened only when he started to appreciate that the question is not who "goes first," but who determines what one wants. Since that power is not based on gender, Rod could accept himself as a boy because he was no longer competing with what he saw as the "preferential position" of girls. While the feminist movement has deplored the forcing of sex roles on boys and girls, a child does need to establish his own gender. If not, for either sex the minimum result, as we have seen, may be an unconscious fear of sexual success.

The World of Things

I knew a violinist who was generally acknowledged as among the best in the world, but who was afraid to plug a lamp or an electric shaver into a wall outlet. The reason was not so obvious as a youthful traumatic experience with an electric shock. Rather, the wall plug had come to represent for him everything he saw in himself as clumsy and incompetent. He could thrill men and women with his artistry, he played a good game of tennis, he was a remarkable conversationalist, but when it came to "things" and money, he was awkward. He had no fear of success so long as he remained in the world of music, ideas, and social relationships, but only of the world of things.

Why do people have trouble with inanimate objects? The answer is that when things are abused, reason tells us we are responsible, but emotionally we transfer our vexations to the things themselves instead.

In "primitive" tribal societies, the social compacts of personal and interpersonal relationships are invariably overlaid with a veneer of materialistic symbolism. Fetishes, taboos, and totems abound. Individuals are told what things they must have and what they must not have. By these devices the world of outward reality—trees, animals, stars—is brought into the tribe and its members are each given a mystic individuality and power that is taken from the outside world.

Similarly, children absorb and digest their outside world. At first they make no distinction between animate and inanimate objects, between personal and material relationships. In fact, most of us never do make that distinction clearly. We talk about "having" a mother and "having" a personality and "having" a nice time or a new pair of shoes—and all with the same verb. Thus when a small boy bruises his thigh on a coffee table, he hits the table and says, "Bad!" When a little girl tries to insult her father, she says, "I hate you, you—you—*thing!*" Or, as one of my small patients said to his mother, "You're just a broken washing machine."

As adults we may "know it's childish," but just the same we feel angry with things when they let us down—a bicycle with a flat tire, for example, an out-of-place piece of furniture in our way, a blouse with an indelible stain. A man I know backed his new Rolls Royce into a tree and dented a fender. He had the dent removed, but then he sold the automobile at a considerable loss because, as he said, "I knew I would never feel the same about it again."

Man, having rid himself of most primitive fears except the fear of eyes, may respond to "things" as he does because they have no eyes and are safe. Millions of years ago, it may be that some prehuman grasped a stick or a rock, eyed it, decided it was harmless, and began throwing it. Sometimes it bounced as a ball bounces, skipped on waves, or rolled on earth. Sometimes it frightened off animals, or hit and stunned them, making them easy to secure. In the process, man held the object, mouthed it, banged it, bent it, and kicked it. Over millions of years he developed hand, eye, and brain simultaneously, and learned to fashion fine artifacts. Ultimately he created the achievements of civilization. That has been the archetypal human pattern. Thus an individual who can't use things and manage tools has a genuine reason to fear failure.

Some children are hampered in their use of things by poor coordination. Generally their parents pay no particular attention to this problem if these children are normal in other respects and respond well to nurturing. For a child, however, dexterity with tools seems tremendously important, and I believe that the lack of it should be treated as carefully as more obvious disabilities. Unless a congenitally awkward child is given a little extra sheltering and training in being competent and feeling confident in his handling of things, I have found he usually grows up with a poor self-image and a deep-seated fear of success, because success is so unfamiliar.

A good example of how useful "things" can be is illustrated in Eddie's story. Last year his mother and father brought this eight-year-old boy to me because they were disturbed about the difficulties he was having in learning to read.

"What have we done wrong?" the father wanted to know. "Eddie's still floored by easy words like 'cat' and 'dog.' My wife reads all the time, and Eddie's brother, Kevin—he's twelve—likes to read too."

"Did you ever have trouble reading?" I asked him.

"No, I can read all right, but my dad couldn't read so good. Is it hereditary?"

"We don't know for sure, but it can run in a family and sometimes skip a generation."

I looked at Mrs. J. She was listening to us quietly.

"Do you see any talent in Eddie, something that has nothing to do with school?" I asked her.

"He's good with his hands," she said.

"Okay then," I said, "let's see if we can't make Eddie feel more useful and more cheerful. Until now, he's felt stupid because he can't read when other children can. We know he's intelligent, but he can't believe it. It's necessary for him to taste success first." I turned to his father. "It's lucky that you're a plumber. Maybe you can take Eddie out on some jobs with you after school. Let him be a father's helper."

Both parents hesitated, but decided to try it. It took only a few months for the results to show. Eddie became a cheerful youngster, proud of his newly developed skill. This success created a sense of well-being in the boy, and he concentrated more and did better in his remedial-reading class at school.

Having served as a bridge between self and society, the "things" and thing relationships that a child has learned will remain a secure base camp for the remainder of his life. Things are good therapy not only in helping a child advance, but also as a bastion to which he can retreat periodically, for whether they are counters in games, or dolls, or security blankets, things represent an inanimate, eyeless, safe universe into which the human being can submerge himself for solace.

A psychiatrist perceives the solace compulsive children find in things when they have transferred all their loves and hates and most of their conversations to their people surrogates. A nursery world of dolls and teddy bears is normal because every child needs a succession of substitutes and intermediaries before he can face the harshness of reality, but the child with no other universe is usually trying to overcome inadequate nurture, bad self-image, and massive attacks of the fear of success.

Martha was a lonely little girl, with a remote working mother who had been deserted years earlier by her alcoholic husband. Martha's most prized possessions were her pets, a pair of gerbils. "I know my gerbils love me," she said, "because they tell me so."

Many of the children I see tell me that their favorite

things talk to them. Most add that there is a difference between the reality of things and that of people. Martha, however, would not admit to that difference. As far as she was concerned, her gerbils really did talk.

The tendency of human beings of all ages to take cover in things has long been used by psychiatrists as a therapeutic aid. Tool therapy, play therapy, or manual therapy (as it is variously called) is a standard method that helps regenerative psychological processes do their healing work. All thing-making or tool-wielding activities—primarily the plastic arts—are beneficial to an old mind in torment or to a young mind balking before one of the jumps in the childhood steeplechase.

Success with material possessions, or the fear of it, builds on a child's experience with day-to-day routines and the rules of the parental home. A child masters the bewildering set of techniques, schedules, and systems associated with the use of things in a hit-or-miss fashion, with many swift spurts and regressions along a broad front. But the basic progression is straightforward. The ability to grasp and wield ideally leads to orderly placement and storage of things, so that they are accessible when they're needed. Neatness in putting things in place ideally leads to neatness of person and in matters of time and scheduling. "Good" schedules and systems may be extended to "good" formal relationships with other people, and then to "good" manners and "good" ethics.

What is loosely called a "security blanket" in everyday speech plays an important role at this time on the social continuum from thing relationships to people relationships. In psychological parlance, a security blanket is a child's favorite toy and bosom companion, which may be a worn blanket, a decrepit stuffed animal, or even a tennis ball or wooden doll: We call it "transitional" because a child hangs on to it from infancy often into the grade-school years and because it helps lead a child to relationships with people. Typically, a child holds it whenever he needs comfort and a source of outside strength, often when he is regressing and healing a psychological hurt.

Half the friendliness of a "transitional object" lies in its familiarity, its texture, its smell, even its taste. To adult eyes, it usually looks more like a dirty, dowdy object than a treasure. But to throw it away, replace it, repair it, or even wash it would be one of the most destructive things a mother could do to her relationship with her child. It would make the child feel not only that she was hostile, but that she set no values on his world. And since she had no respect for that world, the child would have less respect for himself.

Doug's mother was a compulsively clean and orderly woman, as she made clear during her first visit to my office. "I'm telling you, Dr. Tec," she said as she sat stiffly in a straight-back chair, "it's getting impossible in my house." She smoothed her already immaculate dress and I saw that not a hair on her head was out of place.

"You don't know what it is to take care of three children," she complained. "I'm exhausted."

She was still in control, but her face began to twitch as she went on: "I decided recently to clean up the mess. Dougie, you know, is already four, but he was still taking that dirty old rag of a blanket to bed with him. Disgusting! So I took the step. I put it in the washing machine. I really wanted to throw it away, but I was afraid he'd have a temper tantrum. I gave it back to him nice and clean, and you know, he wouldn't touch it. He wanted his other one, he said. I told him it was the same one, but he wouldn't believe me. He insisted that it wasn't and cried half the night. I don't understand."

"To Doug," I said, "the smell and touch of that security blanket changed when you washed it. He doesn't recognize it. To him it really isn't the same. Still, I suggest you leave it with him for a while, and if you're lucky, he may accept it again."

"But I hoped he'd get over this nonsense," she said. "After all, he's four years old."

"Doug obviously needs that blanket," I told her. "It would be normal if he kept it well into grade school. Besides, you've already seen to it that he doesn't take it out of his bed, so why should it embarrass you?"

While she wasn't pleased with my attitude, she was so compulsive that she would never have thought to defy my recommendation, and in subsequent sessions I was able to give her some insight into how flexibility would make her life easier. Doug also got to keep his security blanket.

In our complex, heterogeneous, mobile society, the conventions of life differ greatly from house to house, and the lack of a single cultural standard makes it difficult to enforce family rules whether about transitional objects or other situations. In fact, it is a stock complaint of first-grade teachers that modern children come to school unprepared for academic training because they have not yet learned any rules at home. Tony Smith, for instance, has to go to bed at seven o'clock sharp. Maria Ramirez, on the other hand, has to take a nap in the afternoon, but she is permitted to eat dinner with her parents at nine in the evening. Jane Carpenter has been up for hours before it is time for her to go to kindergarten, but Henry Painter's mother drives him to the same class in her nightgown and polo coat. Each child brags to the other about the good things in his life, and parents hear about how much greener the grass is in some other child's yard.

While it may be true that in a mobile community parents can't say, "This is done and this is not done," as was once the case, they can and should say unequivocally, having agreed beforehand on the rules and standards they want emphasized, "This is how *we* do it." If a child complains that Maria gets to stay up or that Henry doesn't have to report home regularly, the proper answer is, "That's tough. In our family we do thus and so." A firm family pattern, consistently enforced, is accepted by a child and will stand him in good stead in later life.

When a person is able to lead an organized life as an adult, the genesis is in the early experience he had as a child when rules were imposed. If a child grows up without rules, he will have a continual anxiety reaction to the rules and responsibilities that govern adult life. I knew a housewife who grew up without sufficient rules and thus no matter how competent the housekeeper she hires, she can never use her properly because she does not know how to define and structure the help's duties. When she attempts to do this, she experiences an anxiety that is palpable and contagious—and the help walks out as a result.

The easiest specific house rules to teach children are those that can be demonstrated with inanimate props. It isn't difficult to teach a child to use a toothbrush, but it is difficult to teach him to use kindness with a brother or a sister. However, once a child has learned by example and practice to be graceful with a spoon, a hammer, a ball, a button, a clothes hanger, or an automatic salutation, this mechanical expertise can be extended eventually to all sorts of relationships, including those of friendship, salesmanship, even marriage.

Instead of letting a child extend his "thing" relationships gradually and naturally, most of us give children maxims that are too advanced for their emotional and conceptual development. When a parent tells a little girl to "love" her brother or exhorts a little boy not to be "piggy" with his possessions, such urging falls on deaf ears. A child can't be expected to show generosity until he has begun to overcome infantile insecurity about himself. He must first feel safe about his "thing" relationships before he can go on to good relationships with siblings and friends. If, however, because of physical clumsiness or emotional isolation a child is deprived of the gratification that comes from the ability to relate to others, then as an adult, success might be seen as unacceptable because of this earlier experience. Thus, to insure the course of natural development, we should not interfere in a child's territoriality and pride of ownership about his possessions. Only through "selfishness" with them can he prepare himself for displays of "unselfishness" with other people. To question a child's right to keep his own things is to delay development of secure "thing" relationships and put off their extension to social relationships. Additionally, parents who are forever telling their children to share possessions should note that they themselves would be aghast, for example, at the notion of sharing their jewelry with their neighbors. Nor would they expect to share stock-market tips with rivals. Why, then, should children be different?

At least half the fights in families with more than one child are waged over things and ownership. Many of these battles could be avoided by hard and fast laws of property. The house is family property to be shared, and through sharing rooms and furniture, the children get their lessons in sharing. They may share clothes and towels, too, without caring, but toys and tools are something else. These are the 'things" of their personal "thing" universe, and their sovereignty over them must be respected. When it is not, the fear of success manifests itself in the adult who cannot tolerate people's respect because as a child his sovereignty was not respected.

When an elder brother or sister takes away a personal "thing" from a child, impinges on his sovereignty, the child digs in his heels and fights and screams. The typical mother then punishes the aggressor, incidentally reminding the aggrieved one that selfishness is wrong. The punishment is as nonsensical as the admonition. Usually the older brother or sister picked on the child simply to gain attention, and the punishment became the attention. The older child got what he wanted, and the younger child got what he could least use: a sermon on sharing.

Recently I listened to a conversation in my office that was typical of a domestic drama prompted by sibling problems in sharing.

"Chris is eight, you know," said his father, "and Jim is only six, but Chris is constantly on Jim's back. It's true that Jim provokes him, but the amount of aggression that comes out of Chris is incredible."

"I used to fight with my sister," the mother added, "but it never reached such viciousness."

"And how about you?" I asked the father.

"I was an only child," he said, "but I had two cousins and they fought a lot. They were never as mean as Chris and Jim, though."

"How do you handle it?" I asked the mother.

"Well, the boys were playing checkers yesterday, and naturally Jim was not following the rules. Suddenly Chris threw the checkers into Jim's face and punched him and banged him with his fists. Jimmy started to cry, and I ran in from the other room. I was so furious at

Chris I could have killed him. I grabbed him and pulled him away and gave him a good spanking. But he never learns, and this kind of thing just repeats itself. I've told him to stop a hundred times. I've even threatened him with 'Wait till your father gets home,' but he's as bad as ever."

"I can't hit any harder," the father said. "I'd be afraid of really injuring Chris."

"I'd like to explain a few things to you—actually two basic principles," I said. "The first has to do with what we call identification with the aggressor, which means that Chris is beaten by his father and becomes like his father when he beats his brother. The other principle is less known."

"What's that?"

"When you punish Chris, you give him your undivided attention, and in a way you reward him. Instead, I suggest you ignore Chris when he fights, and take Jimmy and comfort him. Pretty soon Chris will realize that he gets less attention when he's mean. Give him your attention when he's good by noticing what he does well. Don't praise him too much—that's hard to take. Just notice the good things."

"Why not praise?" the mother wanted to know.

"Because," I told her, "Chris has a poor self-image and if you praise him, he won't be able to accept it. After months of starvation, a hungry man shouldn't get a big meal right away. Ignore him when he's bad and comfort Jim, but praise Chris in measured doses when he's good."

I also pointed out to the parents that siblings who lock horns without adult intervention are more likely to find a balance between dominance and submission in peer relationships. Then as adults their fear of success in the area of human relationships will be minimal. The give-and-take of personal interaction is familiar territory to them.

Time and Space

Most of us learn the primary lessons about space before we are three years old. Our eyes see in stereoscopic color, and from infancy we can look across a room and gauge its breadth, length, and height. Measuring time, however, is a different matter. For that we have no single organ comparable to eyes. Instead, each of us has a sequenced genetic program, locked in and clocked in with a dozen different body rhythms that, in turn, are responsive to outside stimuli. No wonder philosophers and even theoretical physicists have always been mystical about time!

We seldom think of time as a thing, but it is one, and one of the most difficult a child has to master. It is intimately associated with the fear of success. Both time past and time future are relatively safe, because the past is gone and we can laugh about it, while the future is unsure and we can daydream about it. But the present is always with us, treacherous, unsafe, self-revealing. Only in the present can success be procrastinated, and the fear of it prolonged. Time for self-improvement runs out, however, but not the attendant fear of success.

Most of us hover between past and future, fearing to correct old mistakes until tomorrow and inventing out of past experiences countless excuses for inaction. As far as time present is concerned, my advice is to do something, if only to break the pattern. I believe in doing it now and, if it doesn't work, trying something else tomorrow. There are always so many options open in every life situation. But if there is a fear of success here, a fear that a certain accomplishment may be in some way dangerous, then a rationalization has to be found and time or the lack of it is frequently used.

At the present moment in human history, the relationship between things and time and fear has been made plain collectively as well as individually. Our compulsive, frenetic success with tools has gotten us into trouble with that other great thing, time. The excessive making of things and the creating of wealth for its own sake have resulted in overpopulation and depletion of the earth's potential bounty. As a result, the expectation of collective catastrophe has increased rapidly, particularly among the young, where there is a corresponding rise in the fear of success. "We are running out of time anyway," they say, "so why should we bother to learn how to use it? Why shouldn't we indulge our hangups and fears of success as much as we want?" The survivors of collective catastrophe, of course, will be the ones who know how to manage time as well as tools.

Most children learn to tell time in kindergarten or first grade, but even many of the brightest don't understand the minute hand of the clock until later. My impression is that late-developing clock readers often have an incomplete stage of development behind them that they need time to work out. If they are not given enough time to remain timeless, if they are scheduled too hard and pushed too fast in their areas of good development and confidence, they can make a permanent fear of success out of the stage where they had a hangup.

The proper sequencing and completion of psychological programs is an aspect of time that has had too little attention. Normal sequencing is "arriving on time." Because of our still primitive test-and-remedy programs, many children who follow unusual sequencing in their development also tend to underachieve in everyday punctuality. The child or adult who habitually arrives late usually has failed to reconcile his own biological clock with the schedules of his parental home.

Since the fear and refusal of success always build on symptoms, I treat tardiness on its own terms. Early in my practice I treated a secretary who got out of work at 4:30 in the afternoon. I first scheduled her for 5:15, but she was always late. And always there was an excuse. Sometimes she just "goofed," at other times she was the "victim" of subway breakdowns, or her boss had made "selfish" last-minute demands. I moved her time up to 6:00 and she came at 6:15. I moved her up to 6:45 and she came at 7:00. I put her in my last slot of the day, 7:30, but she regularly arrived at 7:45.

When that happened, I told her, "I don't want you to come on time anymore."

She looked at me in amazement. "Being punctual," I went on, "is like shooting at a target and always expecting to hit the bull's-eye. That's impossible. For one reason or another, your marksmanship is usually off by fifteen minutes. From now on I want you to aim at coming that much earlier. I will look for you at 7:15, and I'll expect you to have fifteen minutes to read in my waiting room. Occasionally you may get in more reading, and occasionally none at all, but at least you will be able to make full use of your time with me, starting at 7:30."

After that she began to arrive so near the scheduled time so often that I was able to use her newfound success, modest as it was, to build further gains.

Just as time is flexible and has different meanings for us, so must scheduling. When to feed the baby, how often to insist on teeth cleaning, at what age a child should have to do without mother's help in taking a bath, the best meal hours for a growing boy or girl, the proper bedtimes, how old a child should be before giving up naps or pacifiers, the problem of bed-wetting—all these are topics of endless debate. But there are no immutable rules in these areas. Children and mothers make up their own in every culture. Thus baths may be taken twice a day or whenever there is a river handy. Teeth may be brushed after every meal or only when there is a piece of sugar cane to gnaw on. Meals can be served at 7:00, 12:00, and 6:00 o'clock sharp, or roughly morning and evening. If you live in the Amazon basin, or if you're a Japanese or an Eskimo, you may insist that your way is the only way, but it doesn't matter to a child. All that matters to children is a degree of rhythm and predictability in the satisfaction of body needs.

A child should go to bed at a time that suits his parents. The preschool child usually needs ten or more hours of sleep a day, because he is driving himself hard and learning strenuously while he's awake. Nighttime solitude, *per se*, is no privation for a child; rather, it is a positive part of each day. If a child needs attention or fears darkness, that is another matter and must be dealt with on its own terms, but it is entirely within the province of parental convenience and authority to set a bedtime and insist on it. And the same authority holds for establishing meal hours, too.

In talking about mealtimes and bedtimes and parental rights to legislate them, we should remember that this right does not extend to a child's own internal individuality. It is legitimate to insist that a child take baths and be inoffensively clean, but too much regimentation about bath hours may quickly violate a child's sense of what is his own business. Still more violative of a child's private body processes and individual chemistry are rules about defecation and urination. The anus, in fact, seems to haunt the minds of many adults, perhaps because the child who has not successfully trained himself after the age of three to have mastery over his anal sphincter gradually develops a self-image of an inferior, dirty person. When he is supposed to perform a clear, precise piece of work as an adult, he may be overwhelmed with anxiety that, unbeknownst to him, relates to this early self-image.

Willy came to my attention through a phone call from his pediatrician, who told me that this bright second-grader was regularly causing himself embarrassment by soiling his pants in school. His parents had tried various kinds of punishment, including spanking, deprivation of television and dessert, but nothing worked.

I met Willy and his parents in my office, and began by saying to the child, "I know how embarrassing and unpleasant it is for you to talk about soiling in your pants."

Willy listened in tense silence. Then his mother said: "You know, Dr. Tec, how upset we get with Willy's problem. If he would only try harder, I'm sure he could be as clean as any other little boy." The father nodded in agreement. Willy stared into space, blank and truculent.

Still speaking to Willy, I said: "I'll try to get this over with as soon as I can. I know how hard it is for you to sit there and listen to all this stuff. Let's begin with one question. How often do you go to make a b.m. on the toilet?"

Willy moved his lips and a whisper came out: "I don't know."

His mother volunteered, "He withholds it for ten days

to two weeks, and all that comes out is seepage. Once it got so impacted it had to be extracted by finger in the hospital. It was hard like stone."

"Maybe Willy simply has what I call 'toilet-seat phobia,' " I said.

"Oh no," his father said, "he does sit on the toilet."

"Do you really?" I asked Willy.

He blushed and beads of sweat stood out on his forehead as he whispered, "Not exactly, I hold onto the toilet seat. I never actually sit on it. I never touch the seat with my bottom."

"Tell me," I asked "would you like me to help you sit on the toilet without fear?"

"I guess—maybe," he said.

Turning to the mother, I said, "All you have to do is spend a few minutes in the bathroom with Willy every day. Let him hold your hand and simply sit without trying to do anything. It may well be that he is afraid to sit comfortably. He has to feel secure and be sure he won't fall in."

"Really!" his father said. "Isn't he a little old for that sort of thing?"

"It sounds a little far-fetched to me, too, Doctor," the mother said.

"I know, but as other methods have failed, there is no harm in trying my way."

As his parents discovered the next day, Willy was indeed afraid to sit on the toilet. He overcame his anxiety about it slowly, until several months after therapy started, he gave up withholding and got over his soiling problem. Once he was able to relax and sit with comfort, everything else took care of itself. His parents had only been concerned with the end result—his stools—as opposed to considering the child's fears of losing something that was his own "treasured possession" and falling into the toilet with it.

Before an individual can move on in his development without too much fear of success, he must be able to resolve earlier issues that have affected his life. When they are even partly resolved at the appropriate stage they no longer interfere, the optimum situation for further development.

4

SCHOOLTIME

Playing Games

Of all the ordeals for a young school child, learning to play games is the most severe for the tentative personality. Any adult who has seen the tears and tantrums provoked by a deck of cards or a checkerboard knows that games are not all fun for a six-year-old. The reason is that at this age games are a proving ground where the weapons to be used in a lifetime of interaction are tried out with ammunition that is psychologically live. The child's eye sees through the camouflage of fun to the serious competitive living that lies beneath.

So innate is the human wish to win that no child can stand losing a game without unhappiness. Every point gained by an opponent deepens a young child's despair. If he loses several times in a row, his expectation of loss increases, and often he persuades himself he may never win. In that case the child may fall back on his dependence upon his mother, who accepts him at his pregame level of development, and he may begin to avoid competition.

From this discussion a mother might conclude that she should not allow her child to play games. While it does a child no good to lose all the time, a normal child can usually learn to play some games well enough to experience the pleasure of winning. A good parent will help the child win, but the performance has to be realistic. No child enjoys playing with a parent who announces his intention of losing or seems bored. Usually, since the parent is bigger and more experienced, the child will accept a handicap system—that is, a head start in a foot race, or a few extra pieces in checkers. In that way an alert child can learn to win.

Games, with all their psychological pitfalls, serve as an important ingredient in growing up in every known society. Moreover, in all societies the major games are either intellectual capture games such as chess and bridge, or physical eye-limb coordination games involving balls or hiding places. In childhood the hiding-place games—blindman's bluff, kick-the-can, hide-and-seek—are significant echoes of an animal past in which the cub learned to track prey or escape predators, and left the mother to do the killing or defensive fighting. Major games such as football, baseball, basketball, tennis, and hockey all involve balls (or a hockey puck) and demand eye-limb coordination. They, too, are references to the past, when training was required of a predator before it could attempt the kill. By contrast, intellectual board and card games are geared for adults, who do not have to risk their lives in the kill, but must plan tactics to assure the "capture" of a piece or a card.

Games with boards and cards remain good tests of intelligence and of the ability to concentrate, while games with balls or hiding places remain fair examinations in physical grace, teamwork, stamina, tactical planning, and eye-limb coordination. In primitive societies, games are used by the adult community much as I.Q. and kinesthetic tests are employed by educational institutions and industrial psychologists in America.

Recently I have been treating a corporation president plagued by pessimism. "You're a man of negative thinking and positive action," I told him. He responded by telling me with the most vivid intensity of his most telling experience—his first game of checkers. He was seven years old and threw himself into every move with ferocious concentration, winning easily while his opponent, another boy, cried and went home angry. When my patient saw his opponent's tears, he felt miserable, and the feeling was repeated over and over during his successful rise to a corporation presidency.

It is clear, then, that both the triumph of winning and the despair of losing can make for the fear of success. If winning turns out to be empty of pleasure, it can destroy the wish to succeed, and if losing turns out to be predictable and repetitious, it can destroy the hope to succeed. But winning without pleasure drives the psyche on to new forms of experience and endeavor, while losing can, at best, only fortify the will to try again. Every loss increases the fear of success and the expectation of failure. Success becomes the unknown land, and the individual prefers unconsciously to stick to the painful but familiar lack-of-success landscape.

Because I believe that games are cultural tests, put to a child early in life to help the elders in diagnosing and prescribing patterns for the child, I believe that parents must pay attention to a child's games and his reactions to them. Children are attracted to games because they are a mixture of reality and fantasy. Games help prepare us to face real issues, provided we see games in their proper perspective—they are good practice but they do not really count.

School Shock

At school, all the fears of success a child has acquired take on a new reality. Now they are the peculiar burdens of an individual engaged in his first "real business of life," outside the inner sanctum of the home. Protected by his family before, the child has lived with family relationships and emotions, until abruptly, for a few hours every day, he has to live on his own and be judged objectively in competition with children from other families and in a new territory.

The six-year-old, for example, can begin to see that the quantity of matter in a ball of clay does not change if the ball is altered in shape or broken into two smaller balls. In short, the child is beginning to think in abstractions and to distinguish between his own point of view and another person's. His brain takes in fresh information, enabling him to process ideas as well as likes, dislikes, and sense images.

This newly switched-on capacity for objective comparison and abstraction enables the average child to take academic instruction in stride. But the same capacity shows a child how he stacks up beside his peers and makes him sensitive to their evaluations. A child who still yearns for affectionate body contact, worries about mother love, or has not yet learned the discipline of rules, inevitably calls attention to himself, and the attention of his peers is seldom charitable.

At that age only some children are capable of befriending and protecting underdogs. Consequently a child with strong fears of success may quickly convince himself that school and other children are not worth cultivating. In the first months at school, he may make himself an outlaw or the member of an outlaw minority. Once that occurs, the child inevitably slows in his development and may become a terror to himself, the classroom, and the family.

These first few weeks of school, then, are a test, even for children with previous experience in nursery schools and kindergartens. Some of those sensitive to stress, the gifted and the ungifted, the cosmopolitan or the parochial, pass the test with anguish, or else fail to pass it. A few go home complaining of nausea and vomiting, while others suffer headaches, stomach cramps, or dizziness. They beg their mothers to protect them from "that bully" or "that mean teacher," and let them stay home a little longer.

Fear of school is more intense in a sensitive child who has had something unsettling in his recent life—a move from one place to another, an illness requiring hospitalization, a death in the family. Any factors that might bring into focus his accumulated fears of success will make him particularly anxious about changes. One of my patients gave me the following account of his school phobia.

"My brother, who was a year older than I, developed leukemia when I was four. I had been very close to my brother since we were nearly the same age and were living in a foreign country. After he went to the hospital I could never again see him alone.

"I had to visit his hospital room with my mother. Everything there seemed too calm and clean. I hated the smell of ether and Lysol in the hospital corridors. One day my mother did not take me with her to the hospital. She came home to tell me my brother was dead. I didn't know what death meant, but it was clear from her manner that I wouldn't be playing with my brother again.

"That fall I entered kindergarten in the States. My sister, who was ten years older, had already taught me the letters of the alphabet, numbers, and colors, so I had no trouble with the curriculum in kindergarten. But during the rest periods I did get into trouble constantly. It was a progressive school, and I was a restless child. Between 1:00 and 2:00 every afternoon the staff brought out cots for us to lie on, to sleep, or just think if we liked. I hated that enforced hour of quiet and the musty, mothball smell of those World War I army cots. They made me think of the hospital and my brother's death. I made a shambles out of several rest periods, until the school threatened to expel me. My parents were dismayed and at a loss, but someone—maybe my older sister—suggested that I count all the numbers up to a million during the rest period. I thought a million was 10,000, and so for the remaining rest periods of that preschool year I occupied myself with working toward an attainable end. One day late in May, I got to 10,000 and went on with 600 or 700 more numbers during the closing weeks of the school year until I got to the end of kindergarten successfully.

"We spent that summer wandering around America, visiting relatives. I interrupted the trip by having to have my tonsils out. In August, my father went back to his archeological work in Greece, and my mother stopped off in England at what proved to be her mother's deathbed. In September, then, I was in England, going to first form rather than first grade. After the first class, during the play period, an oversized redheaded boy led his peers in a pack around the playground, chasing the foreigner Yank. I had a fair opinion of myself and I was reasonably fast on my feet, but just the same I went home that night with a headache, a stomachache, and every other symptom of severe sickness I could conjure. I not only hated school, I was afraid of it.

"My mother was normally an indulgent woman, but in that crisis she let me stay at home for only two days, then she insisted I go back to school and be 'killed' if necessary. It was a question of family honor, she said. The next few weeks were the worst of my life. The red-haired boy called it the game of the fox and hounds. It was played at every recess. If I had accepted my role gracefully and simply run, or if I had stoutly refused and simply sulked, the others probably would have tired of persecuting me. But instead, I played for real—always running, turning, fighting, getting piled on.

"During those weeks of misery, I suffered from a recurring dream in which, whenever I entered the school, it was like reentering the hospital where my brother had disappeared. I could smell ether and Lysol in the corridors. Instead of class roll call, the teacher lined us all up diagonally across the room so that we faced a funnel-shaped object standing in one corner. It was large, white, and smelled of disinfectants.

"In my dream, every member of the class had to dive into the funnel head first. We waited our turns quietly. I couldn't understand why none of the others seemed concerned or asked any questions or tried to run away. When my turn came, I despaired of uttering the protests I felt. I gave a hop and slid down into the tunnel head first. Sometimes the dream stopped right there, in a sense of sleep and oblivion, but sometimes it went on until I came out of the slide on my stomach in another clean, antiseptic room, where a man was standing. He said to me, 'You are now dead.'

"That dream haunted me until it became as unbearable as fox-and-hounds. One morning on the way to school I encountered the redheaded bully standing on a corner with his back toward me. I jumped him, clawed his cheeks, and did my best to dig out his eyes. The blood I drew scared him, and he shook me off and ran away. When he came back to class a week later, he seemed to have a touch of school phobia himself and avoided me.

"I had shed my role as the fox, and I'm proud to say I got rid of fox-and-hounds in that school. During the rest of my time there, we played an ordinary football game during recess."

Such bullying is only the most naked form of persecution that some first-graders encounter, but it is common enough, symbolizing dramatically the persecution these children fear. The child's self-image and self-respect are at stake. Parents have to see both the reality of that fear, along with their wish to have the child stand up for himself. If a child repeatedly fights and loses, he can acquire a conscious expectation of failure, but if he always runs away, he inevitably develops not only a fear of head-on encounters, but a pattern of failure that may mean he avoids success as an unknown experience.

Since children generally benefit from facing fights and from experience on the street, children who are isolated are at a disadvantage. Life with other children, whether it is good, bad, or indifferent, makes it possible to learn human relations through experience. A child who has to be driven several miles to play with his best friend has too much time between play sessions to develop fears or resentments that may interfere with a good relationship, and eventually such a child may feel successful only when alone. Success with other children involves complicated arrangements and time schedules and is therefore avoided.

Besides fear of persecution or poor self-image, school phobia can be caused by all sorts of vague anxieties. Typically, the under-twelve child cannot specify these anxieties. "I don't know why I'm scared," one says, while another states, "Something terrible will happen while I'm in school." Paradoxically, the most easily imagined reason for being afraid of school—failure to do well in academic endeavors—is never a cause of school phobia. On the contrary, the children who fear school most are routinely good scholars. Most perform well even when they're afraid, and none is ever incapable of performing well once the phobia has subsided.

The severity of school phobia varies as greatly as the reasons for it. Some children are petrified if they have to go anywhere near the school, others avoid only certain classes, and still others go to the school but simply loiter there, attending no classes at all. School phobia has so many guises and intensities that ingenuity is necessary to handle it. Every case has to be treated on its own merits by parent, teacher, or therapist, and each case requires considerable resourcefulness. There are two general points worth remembering, however: First, the physical symptoms accompanying school phobia are not less painful and real because they happen to be psychosomatic; secondly, we need to remind ourselves that eventually every child grows out of it. If it is untreated, however, the phobia can add greatly to a child's fear of success.

For my part, I believe the child who fears nursery school should be allowed to stay home because he needs more time with mother. But the child in grade school with this phobia should be encouraged to overcome his fear (sometimes medication will reduce a school-phobic child's anxiety level), because at that point the youngster is advanced enough to cope with the unfamiliar world. Extreme forms of treatment for school phobia are seldom required for children under twelve. The difficult cases are those who develop the phobia in adolescence, since by that time a child has matured enough to appreciate reality, and the phobia then represents a severe form of anxiety that overpowers reality testing.

Andy came to see me when he was eight. He had been out of school, sick with fear, for several weeks. During that school year he had become one of those rare school phobics who perform poorly. He was a daydreamer, getting little out of his work. His parents, who had excellent academic records, could not understand his failure in school. His mother was a withdrawn, preoccupied woman, while his father was a tall, debonair man, much involved in his business career. Andy, a skinny and awkward boy, was oppressed by his parents' constant complaints about his inattention. Things were equally bad at school, where he had been relegated to the "slow" classes.

When I first saw Andy I observed that he was constantly looking out the window, but that he was articulate for his age. And after I asked him what he saw, I found he had exceptional powers of observation and a considerable charm. After a few more sessions I had the impression that he was surrounded at home by a kind of hectic overachievement. Apparently he had never been given the sensuous love and attention he needed.

To light a spark in Andy, I searched for hidden talent and discovered he was musical. His teacher reported that he had a gift for playing the piano. I congratulated Andy on his achievement, but he would have none of it.

He told me it would just make trouble in the family if he learned to play the piano too well because his older brother was already studying the instrument.

Believing that Andy's chief fear of success was his fear of besting the strenuous overachievers around him in his family, I went to his school counselor and advised that, as an experiment, he be moved from the lowest to the highest achievement classes. The counselor was dubious, but agreed to the experiment. Andy immediately responded with enthusiasm. He found himself transported into a world of learning for its own sake. At once he began to contribute to his classes.

At first Andy was secretive at home about his new success in school. He took satisfaction in the scoldings and lectures he got because they were a substitute for the positive love he craved. He feared that if he ceased to be a problem, he wouldn't get any attention at all. But gradually, as he learned he could do everything right at school, he found that he began to get positive attention at home as well.

I worked with his parents and persuaded them to accept his preoccupation and daydreaming. I found that they were not so much jealous of his capacity for success as puzzled by it, since they always had to work so hard for theirs. I also found that at first Andy couldn't accept their praise. I had to show his parents how to give praise to him gradually, in ever-increasing portions, until he was able to digest all their admiration. When that point was reached, he redoubled his efforts to do well.

Sophie was twelve years old when she was referred to me for her school phobia with all the attendant disabilities: dizzy spells, stomachaches, headaches, nausea. Although her behavior was adolescent, she spoke like a younger child. She was a hypersensitive girl, highly intolerant of any kind of stress. Her father was handicapped—he had lost a leg in an automobile accident when he was still an adolescent—and her mother was a bright woman who had abandoned her life and hid her poor self-image in the sacrifice of nursing her husband's disability. Sophie was known in school for her seductive behavior with boys and had already been punished for being caught with a high-school senior.

It took only a little encouragement for Sophie to admit that she didn't like school because she was afraid of the taunts of the other girls, who resented her early evidences of sexuality. In time, however, I could see that she was also insecure in her relationship with her mother and about her own pending womanhood. For years this girl had not been able to turn to anyone for help. She lived in what amounted to an empty house. Her disabled father was not grateful for the attention given him, and the self-squandering mother was too busy presenting her negativism and indecision as sacrifice and idealism. Sophie, in fact, had suffered alone for so long that it took four years for her to gain some kind of perspective on her life, and they were four dreadful years. But at last, partly through maturation and a term in a special school, she began to respond to therapy. Finally, at twenty, Sophie could say that she was free of her school phobia. Recently she wrote me a letter that told about her final resolution of that problem.

"Last summer I decided that I definitely had to do something more constructive with my life, and the local college agreed to enroll me in their lab-technician course. Well, these last months have been the best and most rewarding in my life. My interest in chemistry helped me to become more outgoing in class. I was nervous the first day, but I had a goal and I planned to achieve it. My fears were minimal and they soon subsided. Living in the girls' dorm was the smartest move I ever made. I found that I could make friends easily by showing interest in others instead of being totally wrapped up in myself and my problem. I discovered that other girls have problems too, and by trying to help them I helped myself.

"Last week I began my first research assistantship. I am working for a solid-state physicist and I love it. I am not afraid, because I learned that I am just as human as everyone else. I make mistakes but I do good and helpful things too. I guess that is what life is all about. I still have problems, but the difference is that I have learned to cope with my problems in a constructive way, instead of hiding from them."

When we examine school-phobic children we find they are hypersensitive to criticism and very self-conscious. Success in school threatens them because they believe it is a mistake, and thus they will find at least one teacher or one student who will be critical of them to confirm their self-doubt. A child gets over this school phobia by taking counterphobic measures to develop his self-confidence at school with the help of his parents and teachers.

Dyslexia

While school phobia encompasses a whole range of problems, it does not, as we have noted, include the most obvious reason for a fear of school, difficulty in learning. Instead, that disability is usually given the general term "dyslexia." Dyslexia, which is a reading disability (despite good intelligence) appears to be a congenital disorder of the nervous system. It appears in all degrees of severity, impairing reading ability most noticeably, but also frequently affecting spelling ability and occasionally mathematical ability, and is a powerful cause of the fear of success.

Dyslexic children have an inability to grasp concepts, as though they lacked the necessary mechanisms in their brains to compare, to abstract, and to reproduce thoughts without tremendous effort. Occasionally dyslexic children have trouble telling left from right, and they seem uncertain about which arm to throw with or which leg to step with. They often have a hard time deciding which hand to write with and remembering which way letters go on a page. They may have 20/20 vision, but still find it difficult to settle their gaze and absorb what they see. Sometimes their ears fail them in differentiating between similar sounds, and they have little capacity to interpret the sense of words from elliptical conversations or subtle innuendoes. They frequently have poor control of fine muscles and difficulty in directing a pencil or a spoon. Sometimes they are awkward in large-muscle activities, such as sports. All these signs are not significant unless they come in clusters.

Some dyslexic children are hyperactive and some are above average in intelligence. They often turn out to be highly talented individuals with a large capacity for survival. In a society that requires regular left-to-right scanning and a good deal of other systematic activity, the dyslexic child is at an early disadvantage. If these children can learn to compensate for their disability, however, they may be outstandingly successful.

Almost all dyslexics can be trained in special classes to overcome their learning problems. Until recently they were penalized in most schools by teachers who said,

"You're intelligent, but why don't you try harder?" One might as well tell a blind child to sharpen his wits by walking in traffic. It takes repeated exercises before a dyslexic can learn how to compensate for his learning disabilities. If such a child is not given early help, he will be maimed by a fear of success out of all proportion to his disability, success being the *terra incognita*. That kind of experience was summarized for me by a fourteen-year-old boy.

"To be a dyslexic is to feel different from everyone else and to be constantly ridiculed because you're stupid or you try to cover up your mistakes. People call you stupid and an idiot, and you really begin to wonder whether it's true because so many people say that. Sometimes, if your parents don't know what's wrong, they say, 'What's wrong with you? Don't you care about what you do? Your teacher tells us that you are always fooling around in class.' They say you fool around, but it's because you cover up by being a clown. When you're a dyslexic the way I am it's hard to play the games that the other kids play, like baseball. I have the hardest time catching that stupid ball or hitting and even throwing it. I think it's a lousy game anyway, but I am saying that to protect myself, or so they tell me. That's another thing—everyone likes that game. I can't stand it, so I feel different.

"I talk a lot, and they call that my way out—or hyperactivity, I think. In school I have trouble in English. I also don't get all the directions, like someone will send me to get three things and I'll come back with only two, but one of them wasn't on the list. It is so frustrating to do everything wrong. When they told me that I was dyslexic, first I didn't believe them, but after a while I began realizing that it wasn't my fault for once, and it helps me understand a lot of things. It also helps me to cope with my mistakes, so I guess it's a good thing to know."

Few adults could have put it better. Dyslexic or not, a child at this stage of development hopefully has acquired enough mastery of himself and his school environment that, as a consequence, he can accept his successes without trepidation.

5

THE MATURITY SPIRAL

The Parent-Child Relationship

The fear of growing up, as I mentioned earlier, together with ignorance of how to grow up, can be the chief source of a child's fear of success. During the years from six to thirteen, a child frequently re-evaluates his fears and his feelings about becoming an adult. Every re-evaluation is prompted by some new development in his genetic program of growth, and each time this happens the child has an opportunity to lessen his fears, improve his ability to cope with adult success, and prepare for a life of independence. How well a child takes advantage of these opportunities depends on his interrelated, interacting experiences at home and at school.

Parents at this time in their child's life should accept the fact that, deep within, they have mixed feelings about their child's growth and endowments. Inevitably a child who grows up successfully leaves home and the parents are lonely. Then, too, a mother with a pretty daughter can scarcely escape twinges of jealousy, any more than a competitive father with an able son entirely suppresses the natural urge to outdo him. I once knew a teenager who could have been a baseball superstar but who became a dissatisfied salesman instead. His father, who once had been a brilliant baseball player, slapped his face before a crowd when the boy had carelessly thrown his bat after a hit in a Little League game. The boy had been put off by his father's zealousness about the League, and the slap established in him a fear of successful play, but the father's motivation undoubtedly related to his competitiveness with his son.

Children are often more conscious of ambivalent parental feelings than the parents themselves. I have seen many children who say frankly that they fail in school or play because they fear overshadowing a parent, friend, or sibling. Even more frequently I see children who rob themselves of success in order to hurt their parents and take revenge on them. I hear remarks such as "If I get good marks, Mother will show everyone my report card as if it was hers," or, "I'm not going to make the football team. You think I want Dad marching up and down the station platform wearing me like some kind of medal?"

I had a case recently that illustrates this situation. Mr. B. came to me about his son's unwillingness to play ball with him. "I consider myself a good father," he said, "and I'm glad to play with Keith. He's eight, and it seems to me he should be old enough to be happy and grateful. But on weekends now, whenever I suggest playing catch with him, he says, 'No!' "

Mrs. B., who was with him, said, "You're not telling the full story."

"What do you mean?" he exclaimed harshly.

"Well," she said to me, "at first Keith was very eager

to get out with his father and play ball, but my husband can't just play, he constantly instructs, 'Do this, don't do that.' "

"I want him to learn how to pitch and catch the ball right," Mr. B. said.

"You have to understand," I said, "that children learn by watching their parents. If you stop instructing him, he'll play gladly enough and gradually he'll learn better coordination by watching you."

"That's a point," he admitted. "But I think Keith doesn't want to do it right."

"If you feel that way, he's sure to sense it," I said. "But believe me, if he can play ball without anxiety, for the fun of it, he will eventually enjoy doing it right."

"I don't see how."

"I thought I'd explained already. By watching you. By not using ball playing to get negative attention. He may fear that moderate success in playing catch could lead to future failure. He may think he can't live up to your next demands. When you refrain from coaching and criticizing, Keith will enjoy playing. It takes a lot of self-discipline on your part."

"I've always prided myself on my will power," Mr. B. said. "I'm going to give your miracle cure the test."

How to Talk to Your Child

In order to grow up without developing the destructive fear of success, a child needs no special prophylaxis or pressure from his parents. He simply requires on ongoing, day-by-day dialogue. The content of these conversations matters very little as long as they are varied and spontaneous. I have accumulated a number of simple observations about child-parent dialogues that may be helpful and prevent the fear of success from gaining intensity.

First, and most important, a child seldom knows how to deal with a question that begins with the word "why." These "why" questions rarely start conversations or elicit good responses. Consequently, don't ask, "Why have you come home so late?" The child won't know how to tell you, and in any case, a parent can usually make a shrewd guess. Specific questions, on the other hand, are far more likely to elicit specific answers. Consequently, "What did you tell Johnny about our building a swimming pool?" is more effective than, "Why did you lie to Johnny about the pool you want when you know we can't afford one?" Also the child will always lard his answers to "why" questions with "I don't know," which becomes a regular punctuation in all sentences for those children who are troubled by the impossible "why." Here is the child who is unhappy with camp and is asked "why": "I don't know, it was rainy there. I don't know, the rules were tough. I don't know, some of the kids were mean. I don't know why, I wanted to come home." Obviously he could have specified in detail what was wrong, but faulty questions such as "Why didn't you like camp?" only elicit an "I don't know" response, which represents a fear of successful communication and self-knowledge.

A helpful technique to exorcise "I don't know" works the following way in practice. Talking to a powerful, muscular twelve-year-old named Paul, I asked: "What made you chicken out when Bob slugged you? After all, you're bigger and stronger than he is."

"I don't know, but he's a dirty fighter," Paul said.

"You can figure it out," I said, "but first write down 'I don't know' on a piece of paper."

Paul was puzzled, but he obediently scribbled the words.

"Now," I said, "tear up the piece of paper and throw it in the wastepaper basket."

He looked at me doubtfully, but crumpled the paper and threw it into the basket.

"Fine," I said, "you've thrown those three words away. Try not to use them any more. From now on you'll pretend that there's always a way to figure out a few answers, no matter how hard the question may be."

That was how Paul and I destroyed "I don't know" and began a conversation.

Conversely, when a child asks questions, he wants answers that don't range too widely beyond the scope of the curiosity that prompted the inquiry. "If I ask Dad what time it is," one of my patients said, "he explains to me how the watch was invented." A parent must always feel his way between overanswering and underanswering. Often the phrasing of the question provides a clue. "What time is it?" is obviously no more than a request for information. "How do you know that elephants can swim?" is probably a request for an elaborate answer and a good story.

That doesn't mean, however, that a child has no use for really thoughtful answers. Many of the questions he asks—about life or death, earth or sky, love or hate—are profoundly serious and penetrating and even if the answers are brief, the answers must do justice to the questions. A child who gets nothing but trivial answers may turn out to be as shallow and cynical as those responses.

As the child progresses up the maturity spiral, conversation and shared activities with a parent helps him to overcome fears of success, but the great enemy of this relationship is superficiality, a fear of probing beneath the emotional surface. I have treated highly intelligent people and their children who suffered from fears of successful communication with each other; I have also known engineers who couldn't help their fourth-graders with the new math, and professional football stars who couldn't talk to their children about winning footraces.

Often superficiality in a family relationship is caused by a skeleton in the closet, a family secret.

When Bobby's father came to see me, he looked proper, correct, uptight. He told me his son, his namesake, was having difficulties at school, although he tested well and had no learning disabilities. Still, he was failing seventh grade, and in earlier grades he had never achieved the level of his potential.

Bobby came to talk to me, and I soon found that every response had to be pulled from him as though it were a tooth.

"I don't have any problems," he told me. "I'm working in school, but I get bad marks."

"There's a change in you compared with the way you performed in the fourth and fifth grades, and even the sixth," I said.

"Yes, but it was much easier then."

"Do you think it would be interesting to consider the reasons for your lack of success in school?"

"I don't know if there are any. It just happens that way."

"Well, let's pretend there are reasons and imagine what they might be."

"I told you already," he said. "There aren't any reasons."

"Okay, tell me about your day yesterday. What did you do?"

"Nothing, there wasn't anything to do."

"Don't you have friends?"

"They're all busy or something."

"It was Sunday—usually people like to have some company on Sundays."

"My parents never have anyone. They just watch TV or sleep."

"How about you and your father—do you talk?"

"What's there to talk about? If I want a glass of milk, I know where the refrigerator is. There's nothing, no need."

"And your mother?"

"She's always cleaning or cooking and busy with the baby."

"Don't you have meals together?"

"No, Mom sleeps late or is with the baby, Dad goes to work early, and I don't like breakfast."

"How about dinner?"

"They eat too late. I take a plate and eat in front of the TV."

"Did you ever talk with your father about anything?"

"He tells me to do my homework."

"Does he help you if you need it?"

"No, he doesn't have the time, and anyway, he doesn't know new math."

"And your mother?"

"She's dumb; she wouldn't know."

"I thought your parents were college graduates."

"Yes, but that's different." There was a pause.

"What's your religion?"

"Protestant, I think." He blushed and hesitated. "We don't go to church."

"Any talk about religion at home?"

"No."

"Where are your grandparents?"

"My mother's folks are dead and my father's live in Brooklyn."

"Do they visit you here in the suburbs?"

"No, my father doesn't like them to come. I don't know why. Anyway, how is it going to help me in school if we talk about my grandparents?"

When I saw Bobby's mother, I followed up this clue about religion and grandparents.

"Yes," she said, "you may as well know, my husband is trying to pretend he's not Jewish. He changed his name and he's ashamed of his parents, who keep theirs. He never lets them visit. He's so afraid to be found out, it's pathetic. I think Bobby knows about his father's Jewish origins, but he plays the game. My husband avoids any discussion with him."

"It's possible your husband keeps everything on a very superficial level because he's afraid that any conversation may lead to the discovery of his Jewish background. Does your husband's job depend on his not being Jewish?"

"Not at all, and what's funny, everyone in his office knows. He thinks they don't."

I called Bobby's father and asked him to come in and see me.

"Well," he began, after he sat down in my office, "you've seen Bobby a number of times, but he's still doing very poorly at school."

"Do you talk with him?" I asked.

"I always say, 'How was school?' and 'Did you do your homework?' "

"But do you talk about any subject that's conflict free—not just questions of do's and don'ts?"

"What's there to talk about? He's not interested in me or my work."

"He's intelligent. Did you ever tell him why his grandparents do not visit and why their last name is different?"

"I can see my wife opened her big mouth." He was pale and trembling. "I don't think there's any need to discuss it. I came here to help Bobby."

"One way to help is to stop pretending. Your ethnic background is no secret. You're fooling yourself. Ask your wife. And Bobby is inhibited by it, because it keeps you from talking to him freely."

"There's nothing else to discuss," he said angrily. "Good-bye." He went out, slamming the door.

Two weeks went by. Bobby's paternal grandfather had a stroke and went to the hospital in critical condition. Bobby's mother called me to ask for a family conference. When they arrived, Robert Sr. opened the session.

"I've had to do a lot of thinking the last few days," he said. "I decided to speak freely. Bobby now knows everything."

"Things really are much better," the mother said.

"It's great," Bobby put in.

"What happened?" I asked.

"I'm interested in his work at school," the father said. "He's teaching me the new math."

"Robert and Bobby have some things in common now," the mother said. "They go together to see Grandpa in the hospital."

Nonconversational statements that repeat themselves like defective grooves in a phonograph record will also stultify children. A good example: "You should love your brother, you should love your brother, you should love your brother." I once said to an eleven-year-old girl: "You say you hate your brother and wish him dead. Your mother always sides with him and makes you take the blame. But let's pretend he's dead. Let's play a game. Tell me how it feels. Make believe how it feels to be without him."

She was silent and then she paled as she answered, "Well, maybe I don't really want him dead. He could change, I guess. I mean, it's hard—he's my brother."

"Listen, this is just pretending," I said.

"Sure, I know," she replied, "but I never thought about it that way. The house could get really lonely."

At another time I was talking to Justin, who was ten and felt threatened by his six-year-old sister.

"I wish the creep would disappear," he told me. "Who needs her, anyway? She gets into my things and bothers me. Why doesn't she just go away and vanish? I don't care if she drops dead. If I wasn't afraid of the police I'd kill her myself."

"Pretend that she's actually moved to California to live with your aunt."

"Good riddance."

"How does it feel in the house without her?"

Silence, but I persisted: "Take a look at your life and your house after she's disappeared."

"Why?"

"Because you're only thinking of how to get rid of her. I want to know how it is after she's gone."

There was another long silence, then Justin said: "This is a stupid game. She wouldn't ever move that far away."

"I'm telling you she did," I insisted.

"I wouldn't have anyone to fight with," he admitted, almost in a whisper.

Children are so good at make-believe that this shock

technique of inviting them to see into a possible future can be used in all sorts of fear-of-success contexts. For example, nine-year-old Peter shouted at me: "I don't want to get A's. I'd rather have friends. Only girls get A's. Kids hate me when I get an A."

"Would they like you if you got an F?"

"No, but you don't know how it is. You're not in the class."

"But I'm trying to understand. Let's pretend you really are a lousy student. Can you imagine it?"

"I guess so."

"Would Jack still be your friend?"

"I don't know. He's mainly interested in baseball."

"How about Jeff? Would he like you better?"

"He's mainly interested in his stamps."

"Well, that leaves only Rob then, doesn't it?"

"Yeah, well, I really don't mind Rob so much. He's smart, too."

"He might come to dislike you if you were stupid. Isn't that right?"

"I guess so."

A year later, in fifth grade, Peter was getting all A's and B's. "This year a bunch of the boys are getting pretty good marks," he explained to me. "Not just me and some girls like before. So I don't mind so much."

The technique of pretending can be useful to parents as well. They can pretend how things would be if a child had his way. It makes an effective device for sustaining a healthy parent-child conversation. A variation is for the parent to agree when a child says something outrageous, and at the same time exaggerate in a way the child can understand. For example, a mother hears her son sneer at her under his breath: "Fatso!" and her answer is, "I'm glad you noticed."

The conversation of the home, in fact, should feed on flexibility, humor, and a variety of options, a constant novelty in reactions. If a child gets up grumpy and irritated one morning, obviously itching for trouble, and finally spills milk all over the breakfast table, no good will come of calling him a clumsy idiot. To say nothing and clean up the mess, as prescribed in some handbooks of childcare, may be effective once or twice, but not after several episodes. The child who routinely spills milk at breakfast is testing the ability of his parents to act alive. Sameness of response, even when the response is good, loses its impact by repetition. Here are a few responses a parent might try in this familiar situation: "All right, let's all mop off our places and grab a tray, and take our breakfasts into the living room." "I wonder why you're prejudiced against orange juice. Do you specialize only in spilling milk?" "Oh, dear. Well, I cleaned it up yesterday. This time it's your turn. Please be more careful next time."

As long as the reaction is varied, has some gaiety, and keeps a child's interest, the family conversation during crises can flow on to good effect. Banter and even mild sarcasm can do no harm provided the transactions are alive and fluid. The greatest disillusionment for a child's vivacious mind is wearisome, predictably stereotyped reactions of accusation and exhortation.

Novelty and Creativity

Novelty and creativity—these are the keys to keeping a child alert and positive. If it's raining, for instance, and a child is roaming the house, complaining of "nothing to do," picking fights with the furniture or the cat, the parent might try a specific suggestion: "Draw a cheerful picture, dear." The child may say "no," but he will usually come up with an alternative: "I'll build with my blocks." This advice is better than merely suggesting to the child, "Do something, I'm busy," because it spurs the child to dip into his own creative resources. It moves the child from a passive to an active position, and focuses his attention on one of the most difficult and important lessons of growing up—ingenuity.

Ingenuity is also necessary in dealing with a gifted child. Such a child should never be forced to skip grades in school. Rather, if he grows bored and restless, he needs imaginative stimulation and satisfaction, room to forage on the level he is already exploring at home and at school. Most of the difficult gifted children I see in my practice suffer more from artificiality and overexpectation at home than from understimulation. I think of Roderick—his parents called him Roderick, never Rod—a ten-year-old boy, who was an overfed, overcautious pseudo-adult. At school he was a know-it-all, consequently it was hardly surprising that he had no friendly relationships with his classmates. His fear of success in being his own age was so great that he would not play games, nor could he accept even the prestige he deserved among his peers. He had become depressed, withdrawn, sad, and sullen. Life was a burden.

It took a year of therapy to make a child of him once more and to revive his childish joy in being alive. His parents were my chief obstacle. They feared success for Roderick, they feared that if he was a successful child, then he would not be sufficiently intellectual. It required many sessions to persuade his mother that she had given birth to a child, not to a miniature adult.

Another patient of mine whose parents couldn't accept his immaturity—this time reflected in a late bed-wetting pattern—was an eleven-year-old boy.

"Scott's a big boy now," his father began, "and it seems to me he should be ashamed of himself, wetting the bed at his age."

"I can't help it, Dad," he protested mildly.

"Your eight-year-old brother is dry, and even your six-year-old sister," his mother said.

"Did you wet your bed when you were a child?" I asked the father.

Taken aback by this direct question, he cleared his throat before he answered, "I was given a good beating by my father until I learned not to. Maybe that's what we should be doing, instead of seeing all these doctors."

"But you used to beat Scott for it and it didn't help," his wife reminded him.

"Probably not hard enough," he snapped.

This time Scott was visibly upset. "I wish I could be dry all night," he said.

"It's not your fault," I told him. "You wet your bed because you sleep soundly at night. Your controls go to sleep on you. Up to now," I went on, turning to his parents, "I've always prescribed medication for bed-wetting, but if you're interested, there's a buzzer that awakens a sleeper and conditions him not to wet. It cures bed-wetting permanently in two to four weeks."

"How much does it cost?" the father wanted to know.

"First," I said, "I have to know whether Scott would be interested in trying it."

"Yes!" Scott responded.

"Then, to answer the question, it costs twenty dollars, and you'll use it for only a few weeks."

They decided to buy the device, and two weeks later,

Scott's mother called to say that he had stopped wetting his bed. She was pleased, naturally, but there was something else she wanted to know.

"Isn't bed-wetting a sign of emotional problems?" she inquired.

"Not at all," I assured her, "although some psychoanalysts think so. It causes emotional problems because it upsets the child and the parents. It's true that emotional problems may sometimes make bed-wetting worse, but more often the opposite seems to be true. For instance, children who are anxious about sleeping in unfamiliar surroundings often stop wetting for a day or two until they get used to their new beds."

"Yes, that's true," she said, "because I remember when Scott visited his grandmother he didn't wet for the first three days."

I saw Scott a few times after that, and was delighted to find that the fulfillment of his dream of being "dry all night" had greatly strengthened his self-image. He was rapidly developing self-assurance and seemed to be enjoying life.

If parents make an issue of bed-wetting and a child becomes ashamed of his behavior, it can contribute to his fear of success because it creates strong doubts about the individual's self-control. Thus it prepares the ground for his inability to accept success in other areas. Still, bed-wetting is not fundamentally a psychological problem—I believe it to be a biological problem. A two-week treatment with proper medication stops somnabulists, night-terror victims, and many bed-wetters older than six. It should be added, however, that even without medication, most bed-wetters give up their habit by the time they become teenagers.

And by that time, those children who have arrived

successfully at the adolescent threshhold will not only have developed self-control, but will see themselves as competent in school, able to relate to their peers and to express a moderate rebellion against their parents to establish their emotional independence. When all these factors are present and operating at puberty, it is likely that the transition from childhood to adolescence will occur without severe trauma and that the emerging person will be able to accept the success of his metamorphosis.

6

THE PERILS OF ADOLESCENCE

Adolescent Sexuality

Most of us look back on adolescence with mixed feelings. We were so alive and innocent then, but also so inhibited and guilty. It's hard to remember now whether the energy and excitement of those years made up for the pain of growing into adulthood. Things might have been different if we had known what we know now—that during adolescence we fear success more than at any other time and in that same period have the most opportunity to get over that fear.

Sometime between eleven and fifteen, two genetically programmed body processes overtake us. The "logic circuits" of the brain turn on, enabling us to conceptualize fully and observe reality. At the same time the growth and sex hormones turn on, bringing us to adult stature and fertility. The abruptness and the sequence of these revolutionary changes vary greatly from individual to individual. If we're lucky, the appreciation of reality comes first, followed by the gradual introduction of the growth and sex hormones. For the unlucky, the hormones pour in suddenly and appreciation of reality comes late. But even the luckiest may well find the shock of growth brutal and turn back into themselves, using their new powers of reality perception to rework the experiences and decisions of the past, and either exorcise or emphasize the fears of success that have survived. Sexuality is usually the first concern. At twelve or so, a child feels his gender strongly again, as he did for the first time when he was three or four. But now he sees his parents in a new light, because he is capable of having sexual relations. Parents and children can be seductive, wittingly or unwittingly, and the incidence of sexual episodes between parents and children is higher than most people know or would want to believe. Sometimes irreparable damage is done by these encounters, in others the effects are transitory, and in many the guilt and fear associated with the experiences may create psychological problems in later life. Far more common are the instances of sexual relations between brothers and sisters, ranging all the way from early sex play, a common occurrence, to actual intercourse. The possible consequences of these relationships are infinitely varied.

A young woman complained to me that she was afraid of getting A's in her college courses because she was convinced she didn't deserve them. While she was describing this problem she told me, almost incidentally, that she was also afraid of getting too intimate with her fiancé because he might find out that she was not a virgin. She confessed that when she was six, she had shared a double bed with her thirteen-year-old brother and her fifteen-year-old sister. The older children were having such a good time with each other sexually nearly every night that she finally persuaded her brother to let her join the game. Finally she told her fiancé about her doubts of her virginity and explained the circumstances. When she had intercourse, she discovered that she was indeed a virgin. With that, the door to the past was closed for her and she was able to make a happy marriage.

Quite different is the case of a beautiful, socially prominent woman. In the course of her therapy, I learned that this woman, who had been brought up on a remote ranch, had enjoyed regular sexual relations with her brother from the time she was thirteen until she was seventeen. At that point her brother, who was five years older, got married and moved away. She also married not long afterward and had no difficulty making a successful marriage, unencumbered by the past. The brother, however, divorced his first wife and was now having a stormy relationship with his second.

Often the reason for later emotional storms is that boys appear to have the greater crises as the flood of hormones begins and therefore the more difficult resolutions as well. The main reason is that male children are likely to be more dependent on the mother than females are on their fathers, and the male hormones demand a greater switch from passive to active, from a submissive to an aggressive stance. Girls can enjoy flirting with their fathers and thus partially satisfy the demands of their hormones without transgressing social rules and tribal taboos. Boys, unfortunately, can't satisfy their hormonal urges by any approved activity with their mothers. Even in the most metaphorical way, a boy cannot try on his father's britches.

Generally speaking, adolescents of both sexes appear to fall into two groups: those who respond to early sexuality by following their natural urges in some way or a variety of ways, and those who hold their sexuality at arm's length. The latter sometimes suffer as much from long-delayed experience as the first may from premature experience. It should be added that there are a good many variations within these groups according to socioeconomic levels, religious background, and other factors. There are, in fact, innumerable gradations of sexual adaptation. All are appropriate as long as they do not compound fears of success with fears of sex.

Attitudes toward adolescent sexuality have changed markedly in the last decade or so. Sexual behavior in preadolescent or early-adolescent girls was considered delinquent not so long ago. Today it is the violence in this age group, among both boys and girls, that concerns us more. There are many citizens who are convinced that we live in a wildly permissive society where sex is concerned and "anything goes," as they are fond of saying. But the most recent studies by sex therapists show that there is relatively little change in actual sexual behavior. What has changed is the acceptance of this behavior by the children themselves and, to a surprising extent, by the adult population, with a consequent erosion of traditional feelings of fear and guilt.

Most children, of course, react to their surging hormones at adolescence by putting off as long as possible the necessity to make any decisions about the changes they feel in themselves. Growth is an effort, and effort at any stage of life is followed by a letdown. Consequently, children buy time for rest after growth and for thought after realization. They do it by a variety of subterfuges. A boy, for example, may be six feet tall but still see himself as a four-foot child, while a girl may look like Elizabeth Taylor but continue to think of herself as Shirley Temple.

Girls often buy time by talking a lot and by being excessively frank. Twelve-year-olds, for example, are likely to talk a great deal in order to give themselves something to do while they're thinking, and also to try out their new reality perceptions to see what effect they might have. "Do you feel clumsy?" one of these girls says to her elder sister's boyfriend when he spills the gravy at dinner. "Aren't you afraid you'll drop it?" she asks him when he lights a cigarette. At another time, in front of her mother, she says to her father, "Daddy, I'll bet you work late so often because it's more comfortable in the office than here."

Boys usually buy time by other means. A father who came to see me with his fifteen-year-old son demonstrated that fact when he said to the boy: "Norm, if you didn't get into trouble stealing and bullying younger kids and setting off firecrackers, Mom and I would get interested in your school work. This way we don't, and so nobody pays attention to what you should be doing, only to what you shouldn't be doing."

Not all boys go so far as Norm, of course. The less troublesome ones buy time by fixing up their rooms as hiding places, going out in boats, wandering in woodlands, lingering in alleys and garages, or just hanging out in places where they have similar company. Boys who buy time regularly insist upon impermanence as a way of life. "Why should I fix my bike?" they say, "it's old-fashioned. Besides, I'd like to get a ten-speed one." Girls may have a greater yearning for permanence, but they, too, seldom feel ready to accept lifelong commitments. "I don't deserve a good life," said one. "Nothing lasts forever; so when I'm unhappy, I have nothing to fear. The danger is when I'm happy. When things go well, who knows what might happen?" A sixteen-year-old observed: "I always end up with the kind of boy who can promise me eternal love for one night. I think maybe that's what I want."

A New Psyche

Both boys and girls seek to put their parents at arm's length at this time in order to figure out what their new togetherness should be. Schopenhauer described this situation with a parable: "A company of porcupines crowded themselves very close together one cold winter's day so as to profit by one another's warmth and so save themselves from being frozen to death. But soon they felt one another's quills, which induced them to separate again. And now, when the need for warmth brought them nearer together again, the second evil arose once more, so that they were driven backward and forward from one trouble to the other, until they had discovered a mean distance at which they could most tolerably exist."

There is no end to the devices, both ingenious and obvious, by which adolescents mark their disengagement from family participation. An example is a thirteen-year-old boy who covered his and his brother's rooms with scenes of World War II aerial dogfights. These frescoes, which he did himself with some skill, convinced his parents that he must be heading for a career as an artist, but after two years of it, when he had finished taking stock of himself, he gave up art completely. He had wanted occupational therapy and time alone. The frescoes accomplished both objectives.

The diversions children manufacture while they are trying to sort out the world in early adolescence are entirely normal and healthy. They are prompted, however, by hesitancy about growing up, a hesitancy that can easily be twisted into fear of adulthood and fear of success. Parents frequently make two common mistakes at this time. They think they should intrude on their children's "loneliness," while at the same time they are confused about their children, who now look grown-up. To feel lonely and to be alone are quite different states. At this age a child is often too preoccupied in redecorating his psyche to feel lonely or want company. He wants to be alone to think, and while he's thinking he resists all intrusions and demands made upon him. The most intrusive and destructive demand can be the parental insistence that he start acting according to his stage of physical development. Some parents assume that because their children look grown and have become articulate, they should be given a say in the family government. The teenager doesn't need this added demand; he has more than enough to do working out his speculations about himself. More than ever now the adolescent needs rules, because he is looking for some fixed compass point as he draws his ever-widening circles away from home. Children without a fixed home base at this stage tend to glorify impermanence. They talk about a "real me" that is undefinable because they haven't yet had the chance to define it either within the home or by doing anything of significance in the wider world.

When parents complain that their children seem to be trying to build independence on quicksand, the children say: "You don't understand. I want to be loved for my own sake, not for anything I do." If the parents praise them for looking nice or dressing well, they answer again: "That's not the real me. Why can't you see what I really am?" As in earlier childhood, personal praise can be as unacceptable as personal blame. Thus it is better to say, "That's a nice sweater," than to say, "You look beautiful in that sweater."

Of the many adolescents I have seen, Joe best expressed the typical feelings. As a child suffering from tuberculosis of the bone, Joe had been in an orthopedic cast for years. Consequently, at seventeen he was still so puny he couldn't see an adult identity for himself. He came to me because he had just gone through a trip on LSD and had been referred to me for emergency psychiatric treatment. As he talked, it was apparent that acid, age, intellect, and the misfortune of being a misfit had combined to create an articulate awareness in Joe of the adolescent growth-spurt trauma. Some of what he said provides an illuminating insight into the adolescent mind.

"One of the most important things I learned from my drug experience," Joe said, "was about time. Basically, time isn't a continuous thing, where one moment comes, then the next moment, while the last moment is destroyed and no longer exists. Every moment always exists in a kind of complete 'now.' When I'm looking at you moving around in a room right now, I see you move from one position to another. Once you've moved, the other position you were in just disappears and no longer exists. But when you're on acid, you see several moments at one time. If you moved across the room, I'd see you at both ends of your movements, when you started and when you finished and everything in between, in a series of transparent images. They'd extend out from you and I'd see them at right angles, three-dimensional. You see, you feel kind of displaced and at a distance from everything, and you see it going on out there.

"You get this eerie feeling. Time goes by very slowly, endlessly, so you really do feel like you've experienced an unimaginably long time, but only a half hour has passed. When I flipped out, I remember the experience of being for an eternity, an unimaginably long period of time, stuck in one small molecule, one small part of everything. I saw myself coming to the end and the beginning of my life. There's a great deal of beauty, joy, and affirmation, and also suffering. There's a point where you make this discovery about time, and then for some reason you suddenly see there's nothing to be afraid of. It's completely all right. Then there's the most complete feeling of invulnerability, joy, happiness, and security I've ever felt.

"I've seen that life is endless. There is no rest or peace. Everyone yearns for death in some way. At least I do. I yearn for peace, for an end to all struggle and fear. But once you see life is endless, you just go through lifetime after lifetime, never ending—not only you, but other people, too. You see the line between yourself and other people completely. You see that you're all part of the same being."

For all his insight, it will take Joe years to work out his acute fears of growing up. In the two years after I first saw him, he grew dramatically from a runt into a man whom women found attractive, but he had only the most ambiguous feelings of sexual identification, confessing to both homosexual and heterosexual fantasies. In real life he thought he might begin his sex life with a homosexual experience and then move on "from my narcissism" to heterosexuality.

The Mirror Image

The narcissism Joe talked about occurs in a more commonplace way in the familiar adolescent preoccupation with the mirror, resulting in long and frequent trips to the bathroom. Seeking to try on "costumes" that may strengthen what these adolescents find in themselves, they say in effect, "Mirror, mirror on the wall, how do I look?" To which the mirror replies, "You would look okay today if you move your hair to the other side." Parents are often impatient with these lengthy trips. But the adolescent has to evaluate and develop his "costume" for himself, and quick criticism can prevent him from ever arriving at a satisfactory image of himself.

Not to know what you look like, or what you want to look like, may obviously aggravate an individual's fear of success by contributing to uncertainty about what he is and what he wants to be. Training in self-observation can be of great use to many fourteen- and fifteen-year-olds. The mirror test, in fact, is a good way to evaluate the progress of people of any age. If a good-looking person feels uneasy with his reflection in the mirror, he has some fear of success. When he likes what he sees, he is demonstrating that he is not afraid to feel successful.

Hair is by far the most satisfactory part of the body to experiment with in front of the mirror. Hair can be cut, grown, curled, straightened, combed, tied, and molded at will. For the adolescent who suddenly has realized that body changes occur in spite of his wishes, hair can be a last resort of mastery. No wonder adolescents have always played with their hair and in our frenetic and uncertain times have elevated it to a national preoccupation, even a universal symbol of contemporary adolescence.

Adolescents quickly attach to their body image a great many attitudes that stay with them for life. At first they are not real personality traits but extensions of the image to things outside the body. After projecting herself into lipstick or eye makeup, for example, a girl proceeds to identify her "real self" with certain favorite clothes and eventually with the image reflected in the eyes of her first love. Before that time, however, the projection often involves a favorite animal, particularly horses in the case of early adolescent girls, although it may just as well be dogs, kittens, or guinea pigs.

Boys, too, after fiddling with their hair, generally move on to more self-committing but also transitional manifestations of their masculinity. Where girls choose lipsticks and totemic animals, boys return to pre-agricultural hunting days and choose weapons and tool styles. In the days of the Capulets and the Montagues, young Romeo extended his body image directly through his arm into the blade of his sword. Among members of inner-city gangs today, the arm may still be armed, but now it is a switchblade. Most teenage boys, however, select a more approved tool that may be no less lethal, an extension through the leg to wheels and a thrust on the accelerator.

Adolescents set themselves trials of strength and daring in order to prove themselves grown. Only in this way can many of them get rid of their four-foot-high self-images. In boys, these modern self-initiation rites often take the form of "playing chicken" with automobiles, but the same self-proving urge arises in girls. In a large suburban high school, attended mostly by children of well-to-do white Protestant families, there is a ninth-grade girls' club that calls itself the "Black Boy Firsters." The girls in it are all white and have pledged themselves to lose their virginity to a black boy. Not many will realize that aim, but the club nevertheless exists as a bragging point.

Girls often use talking in the same way boys use weapons or cars to reinforce their formative adolescent opinions of themselves, and this overuse of language is also sometimes a symptom of the fear of success. The most extreme case of overcommunication I ever encountered in a girl occurred in Ellen, who feared the success of permanent relationships, since she identified permanency with the destructive model she saw in her parents.

This seventeen-year-old talked incessantly with the frankness of a six-year-old. She was all vitality and exuberance—and conversation. On an errand for her mother to the supermarket, she would get as far as the garage door and come back to ask, "Don't you need tomatoes, too?" Halfway out the driveway, she would call back, "How about cucumbers?" Parking the car in the street in front of the house, she would come back into the house and say, "Hey, I forgot to tell you. You know that TV show I sat up watching last night? Well, the guy finally . . ."

During one of our conversations Ellen described a recent trip to Florida: "I was staying in this motel and I met two guys. I liked George, but Rick liked me. I went with George to his room. Later he says this Rick guy, who also likes me, is his friend with whom he shares things. I played dumb and he explained a bit, but I said, 'No dice.' Then there comes this knocking on the door, and Rick walks in, undressing along the way. I jump out of bed and grab my jeans and sweatshirt and get the hell out. They didn't try to stop me. They thought I'd be game. I'd given them the wrong signal or something without knowing.

"Next morning I was up early, in the dining room, and only one couple was there. I did a funny thing. I said I was lonely and sat down with them, complete strangers, and I told them the whole story, everything that happened. I had to tell someone."

"It's good to have a chance to talk things out," I said, "but with total strangers?"

"They were sympathetic," she said, "and I knew I'd never see them again."

"Maybe they were just polite."

At that she burst into tears and reached for the box of tissues on my office table.

"I would have cracked open if I hadn't told someone."

"You told your mother about that guy in the bar, too," I said, "and there were others. Mother is better than strangers, but you don't have to tell the whole world. You deserve some privacy, don't you?"

"I want to," she wept. "I have to."

"Why don't you write it in a diary when you're alone?"

"I can't write."

"It's not for publication. Even you don't have to read it. Writing is solace, and sometimes it works."

"Okay, I'll try it," she said.

Afterward, Ellen told me her diary provided a wonderful outlet for her emotions and that she felt successfully in control of herself for the first time.

Academics, Athletics, and Acquaintances

One manifestation of the adolescent fear of success that both boys and girls share is the fear of academic excellence. It is different at this stage than earlier because of the girls' emerging sexuality and the boy's now acute concern for friendship. The girls explain that boys don't like smart girls, and the boys often say they lose friends if they do too well in school. Neither statement is objectively true.

"I always do bad on exams," Liz, a pretty fifteen-year-old blonde, told me. "I study hard, I know my stuff, but then something happens. I get into the exam and suddenly I can't organize my thinking. So I disappoint myself and my teachers."

"Your mind goes blank?"

"Not blank exactly, but like it's in a daze or a day-dream. I end up without enough time and as if the whole thing was a flop."

"Do you work late preparing the night before?"

"Of course. There's so much. I could never finish it before 2:00 in the morning."

"Would you run until 2:00 A.M. the night before you had to compete in a race in competition?"

"That's different."

"Not really. The brain suffers from fatigue just as much as leg muscles. If you want to go into training for an exam, you have to start practicing in advance, then get a good night's sleep the night before the event. That's what athletes do."

"My sister does it, too. She's the brain in the family. But that's her way. I do it differently."

"Don't you want to outshine her?"

"I never could."

"Why?"

"She's my big sister."

During the following two months I persuaded Liz that her big sister, her boyfriends, and her parents would not mind if she did well on exams, and even if they did, that wasn't enough of a reason to avoid success.

By contrast, sixteen-year-old Sam never ran out of time on exams. He buzzed through them and turned them in before the time was up. Yet he never did so well as he expected. Before he took his preliminary student aptitude tests for college entrance, known as PSAT's, he asked me how to do better on exams. "It's more important this time," he said. "It means more and I'm getting worried."

"As I remember," I reminded him, "you used to get disgusted with your tests last year and wouldn't look them over. You said they reminded you of something dirty."

"Yeah, I want to show off, I want to be first turning in my exam. But I also can't stand looking through it. I don't ever want to handle it again after I'm finished."

"Like the time when you were six and got whipped for smearing the walls of the bathroom."

He scowled, laughed, and scowled again. "Okay," he said, "I have to treat myself better. I have to start looking at my products—even my tests—as something that's not shitty anymore."

"Tomorrow is only practice," I said. "After the PSAT's are the SAT's, and those are what you're preparing for. Tomorrow you may prefer to go over your answers when you're finished. Why don't you free yourself to stay until the alloted time?"

"But if I think too long, I sometimes correct a good answer and make it wrong."

"You might sometimes, but chances are that most of the time you'll make an improvement."

"I'll do my best."

"Remember," I added, as I saw him out the door, "this is only preliminary. You'll have time to practice my technique before you try the real SAT's."

He did well next morning, and even better when he took his SAT's a year later.

Fear of athletic excellence is another common aspect of the adolescent fear of success. Ginny, for example, was a fine swimmer and diver. Both she and her older sister were members of a water-ballet troupe, recruited from the high schools of their suburban area. She excelled in the sport and was often in the spotlight, but after a single season she dropped out of the troupe.

"I loved it," she said, "but I was competing heavily with my sister. I didn't want to beat her, so I left the ballet and she stayed."

I think, too, of Ian and Bruce, brothers only a year apart in age who hung together to protect themselves from the demands of their intense mother. They conspired to please her, cheer her, and lighten the household atmosphere, but beneath their cooperation they had their own natural sibling rivalry. Fifteen-year-old Ian was tall, handsome, articulate, and grown up. Sixteen-year-old Bruce was stocky, squat, but also good-looking. Although he was intelligent, he had lost a year of grade school during his parents' divorce, and then became a part of Ian's class. The only area of excellence he had all to himself was swimming. Even in that, however, he was the number-three man on his high-school team.

"If I wanted to, I could beat the number-one and number-two guys," he told me.

"How do you know if you've never done it?" I asked.

"Well, I never finish as tired as they do. I have the extra kick in me. But somehow in meets I always hang back until it's a little too late. It's funny. Basically, I think I'm scared to come in first."

"Because at home, in being friends with your brother, you've conditioned yourself to accept second place."

"Maybe," he admitted.

"All right," I said, "then let's consider the options. You can make an all-out effort in swimming and become number one there. Or you can start competing with Ian at home at the risk of spoiling your good relationship with him. Or you can look for new avenues of success that won't conflict with any of your memories about the past. How about wrestling, for instance? You're built for it. Have you ever tried it?"

When I next saw Bruce, he had tried out for his school wrestling team and made it. In two months he was winning meets. By spring he didn't seem to mind being ahead of his younger brother, he had a girlfriend, and he had gained greatly in self-confidence.

Sociability

The fear of being a first-class citizen, a number-one competitor, runs so strongly during adolescence that most children take cover by joining a group, thereby avoiding responsibility for full individuality. Modern teenagers, of course, tend to scorn the old fraternal organizations and talk of belonging only to their own group—to the adolescent subculture in general, and to their own club of friends in particular. The sense of belonging to a social minority, with its own set of values, begins to be especially important to teenagers in midadolescence, when they are trying on the idea of leaving their parents to make lives of their own. Fifteen or sixteen is the normal age for this development, this first willingness to try being free and independent. In most societies it coincides with an adult recognition that the child has reached a new level of development where he must begin to decide for himself. In many states sixteen is the age at which a teenager can get a license to drive, can leave school, and can get permanent working papers.

By this time, most boys and girls have established an

identity for themselves within their group. They have found friends among their peers. However, most teenagers need someone even more special—a "soul mate." A brother, sister, mother, or father is usually not enough, nor is a friend of the same sex. Thus many adolescents find their best companions and therapists in members of the opposite sex. Boys and girls need each other in adolescence as status symbols within their peer group and as an extension of themselves. Through a member of the opposite sex of the same age, a boy broadens his concept of women to include nonfamily, nontaboo representation. Through a boyfriend, a girl similarly broadens her appreciation of the male half of the species. Adolescent boy-girl relationships may not be open-eyed or objective, but they serve to bring the two sexes into the same world. They can be complete trial marriages, including sex, but they don't have to be. More important, the relationship should be an experiment in understanding. Through it, both partners can learn to visualize marriage, and the kind of partner they can live with compatibly.

In adolescence, as at any other time in life, two people of the opposite sex can complement and strengthen one another. But boys and girls are afraid of being number one; both fear the prospect of having to stand on their own and of doing without their parents and siblings. By talking over their mother-love, father-hate, and father-love, mother-hate, a boy and a girl can diminish their fear of success with the other sex.

Unlike the society of adults, the teenage culture accepts newcomers and permits a greater mix of people. Teenagers can welcome companions from outside the class or ethnic background of their parents. Their tolerant attitude enables them to sample a broad spectrum of humanity, and thus to decide where they fit. Through acceptance of chance acquaintances rather than selected ones, a teenager learns to expect little of friends and much of self. These aphorisms may sound cynical, but they are good antidotes against disillusionment and aggravated fears of success in later life.

Sixteen-year-old Helen, however, did not know where she fitted in terms of either friends or family when she first came to see me. Her father, who had been accustomed to beating her mother regularly, had left home. As though to replace him, she had taken to assaulting her mother with her fists and was inflicting almost as many bruises as her father had.

Helen talked like a machine gun, her voice abrupt and staccato, the words coming out with force. Helen had just tried to commit suicide with an overdose of aspirin.

"I knew very well those aspirin wouldn't kill me," she began.

"So why the effort?" I asked.

"Try to understand my position," she said. "Daddy left with that chick who was my mother's best friend. He used to spank me for lying, but he lied to my mother."

"You wanted to punish your father?"

"I don't know. Everything was piling up, school was too much of a drag. Mother was getting on my nerves, my brother is a jerk."

"How about your boyfriend?"

"Which one, the one from yesterday or the one from today?"

"Are there really that many?"

"Why not? It's woman power."

"If it were that good," I said, "it wouldn't have to be that hectic."

"I have a machine inside me," Helen said, "and it propels me into action, never lets me stop."

"Day and night?"

"Especially night."

"You may want to give up speed," I said.

"Who told you?" she shot back defiantly.

"No one but you when you said, 'Especially at night.' I've heard that pattern a thousand times."

Helen looked down at the floor, and her voice was sad and flat. "Okay, once in a while I want to give up speed. Okay?"

"Before you took the aspirin, how many nights did you go without sleeping?"

"None." Helen smiled. "I slept fine. I slept every night—and every night with a different guy." She laughed.

"All right, let's cross that question off the record. My mistake for asking a question when the answer was obvious."

She seemed mollified.

"Let me tell you, I can be good," Helen said. "That's what I tell all you guys. My friends know it. It's no secret. Only my stupid parents don't know it."

"They don't know the details, but they know enough to worry."

"Well, their worry won't help me find out who I am. Where's my home? Is it my father's or my mother's, or maybe I belong in the zoo?"

"In the zoo as what?"

"As a cross between an elephant and a chimp. That's me."

"Someday soon I hope you'll be able to look at yourself and see what others do. Personally, I see quite a bit of good in you," I said.

"Thanks," Helen said, "but I have to see it myself. I don't want to be like my father or mother. I want to change and I will."

Helen was overly optimistic. It isn't easy to blend good resolutions with action, and she had many more ups and downs before she opened a session two years later by saying, "I have syphilis."

"How do you know?" I asked.

"Chuck has it and he gave it to me. I don't see him anymore."

"Have you seen a doctor?"

"No. I thought you might give me a shot of penicillin. I don't want my mother to know."

"First we have to be sure of the diagnosis," I said. "I'll send you to Dr. C."

Helen agreed reluctantly, and a few days afterward I had a call from Dr. C. "I've had a lot of patients in my time," he told me, "but this girl you sent me is the first I've ever seen who wasn't happy to hear she doesn't have syphilis."

Next week Helen began her session with me as though nothing had happened. She seemed bored, in fact.

"Life's a drag," she said. "Same people every day."

Sensing she was in a state of calm that might well be the prelude to a storm, I said nothing.

"Why are you so silent?" she demanded. "Are you playing analyst? Should I go to the couch?"

"You don't need a couch," I said. "What you need is more self-respect. When will you enjoy your own thoughts and stop being bored?"

"Now all of a sudden you're talking too much."

"I can see today is not my day. It's hard to please you. You're on edge."

Helen yawned and stretched her arms. "I'm sleepy," she said. "It's too quiet in your office. Why don't you have some rock music to liven it up? Don't be such a stuffed shirt." She sprawled over the arm of her chair, resting her feet on the seat of the chair next to her. Sixty seconds of silence went by, then she tossed her bomb.

"Incidentally," she said, "I'm pregnant."

"Who examined you?"

"Nobody. I just know. I missed my period. It's been two weeks."

I reached for a prescription pad and began writing.

"What are you writing?"

"An order for a urine test at the hospital lab."

"I know I'm pregnant."

"Let's have a test anyway."

"I don't want to waste the money."

"What do you want, Helen?" I asked, putting down the pen.

"If I only knew, it would be great."

Her urine test was negative; she was not pregnant. A few days after that she came to my office for her regular session.

"It's nice weather," she began.

"But dull conversation," I responded. "If you would only invest yourself and talk beyond immediate events, you might find better conversations and firmer friendships."

"Another speech. Just like my father."

"Try it."

"I might, if you could tell me how."

"For a starter, next time you have something that has high priority, speak about it. First to me. Gradually, you'll learn how to share some of your thoughts with friends."

As time went on, Helen's life became less hectic. She went to boarding school, lived with her grandparents, her father and stepmother, and finally returned to her mother's, the original place. She didn't need to push her mother around anymore and was content to accept her own room as her territory. Nor was she afraid to hurt her father's feelings by having a good rapport with her mother, and conversely, she did not fear offending her mother by having a positive relationship with her father and his wife. Helen had found her place.

Fourteen-year-old Donald had to learn where he fitted in life, too. In one of his dreams he climbed a flagpole and near the top "creamed in his jeans," as he put it. Nevertheless he reached the top where he found a pair of trousers flying like a flag. They were too small for him; Donald is an overweight boy.

"You were feeling too big for your britches," I told him when I heard his dream.

"No, I wasn't," he said. "They were too small for me."

"Have you beaten up your father lately?" I asked.

"You know I haven't," he said. "Last Saturday he picked me up and tossed me halfway across the living room."

Donald's father operated a heavy modern machine, and in his spare time he drank. Sporadically separated for years from Donald's mother, he continued to come in and go out of the family with brutal assertion. The mother was a wispy woman with little self-confidence. Overweight Donald was unsure of himself because he literally couldn't fit into his father's britches, as the dream symbolized, and he was afraid he wouldn't be able to fill them figuratively either. The britches were too small, and he wanted to see his father smaller.

I asked Donald about his fear of success.

"This might not exactly be it," he said, "but let's just suppose it has to do a lot with negative attitudes, attitudes about doing something. For me it goes like this: Suppose you're running in a meet. You say before the race, even if you know you're the best runner in the whole race and you know you can wipe the others out, you say, 'I can't do it.' So if you lose, it's okay, and if you win it's okay, but if you win, you know the others will hate you."

"It's a good example," I said.

Donald went on to give another example. "Let's say you have this friend who likes this girl a lot. So you try to fix him up with her. But you're afraid you're going to succeed in fixing those two up, and you know if you fix them up, you won't be able to get this girl. That could be one fear of success, if the success of what you're doing is not going to work out to your liking."

"How about adults you know? Parents?"

"My mother takes a very positive attitude. She always looks on the bright side of things, really. But my dad—we think he's being extra mean to Mom because he doesn't have any grounds for a divorce. He thinks if he's extra mean to her, she'll say, 'Oh, I hate him,' and file suit for divorce. Then he's got it made."

"He's afraid of a successful reconciliation—that's his fear of success?

"Probably."

"What would you want?"

"Actually I don't like the guy at all. Well, I like him, you know, just because he happens to be my father. But I don't have a real lot of feeling toward him. He always thinks I'm trying to be a wiseass."

"Even now?"

"Yeah, because the other day in the car I worded something wrong. He just got a brand-new car with power steering, and it was a big thing for him because he's only had VWs since about 1960. I said, 'You're not used to power steering, are you? You haven't had it.' He thought I was saying, 'You're driving funny. You're not used to power steering, are you?' And that's why he thinks I'm a wiseass."

"But you didn't mean to be."

"I wasn't intending to be, but it came out that way. I could have worded it better. I could have said, 'You've never had power steering before, have you?' Instead, I said, 'You're not used to it.' I just used the wrong words and he jumped on me. My mother could see both sides and she pointed that out to me."

"If you wanted a successful relationship with your father, you could also have said, 'I'm glad you've got a car with power steering. It's so comfortable.' "

"Yeah, well, he was driving funny, though."

"Would you like to have a more successful relationship with him? Or should we rephrase it: Are you afraid of a successful relationship with your father?"

"Yeah. I don't like the guy. If I had a successful relationship with him, like he was my father, living in our house again, I'd be afraid of him. That's the thing. There've been lots of times I've been shaking in my boots."

"When you were little?"

"No, when I was big," Donald said laughing.

At our next session, Donald and I talked mainly about his favorite car. "We were coming back from New York State, boozed up," he said, "and this car went by. I call it my car. It was an Olds 442, and we started chasing it. We were doing ninety miles an hour before we started catching up with it. And there's this guy I know slightly, he's just cruising along at eighty-five. So we come up on him, and at first he slows down 'cause he thinks we're pigs, and then, swoop, he's passed us and we never see him again. A '66 Olds—pretty soon, when I have 800 dollars all in fifties and twenties, I'm going to go up there and slap them on the table, and say, 'Hey! I want your car.' And you know, he's going to say, 'You got yourself a deal!'"

"Aren't there any other cars you'd rather have?"

"Sure, I wouldn't mind having a brand-new Chevelle, built up, you know. But that Olds is a good model for a car. A lot of people keep cars for transportation. I think a car is a thing of beauty."

Having talked about family and cars, Donald and I next passed on to fighting. He believed in several Oriental disciplines, including karate and kung fu. He read about these methods of fighting and even dreamed about them.

"Did you ever feel powerful in your real life?" I asked.

"Yes, now and then," he said.

"With whom?" I asked.

"With myself."

"When you were fighting or when you were alone?"

"When I'm fighting. If I'm winning, I feel very powerful. Don't tell my father, but one fight I had was the last time I went up to his house. A guy about my age or a little older came up and started in with me."

"How did he start?"

"He came up to me and said, 'What are you doing here?,' you know. 'I'm walking around, what's it to you?' I say. I don't really look for trouble usually, but trouble finds me. He says, 'I don't like you.' I say, 'Tough shit. That's your prerogative, buddy, but don't try anything.' So next I say, 'Get the fuck out!' and he goes, 'Yeah, yeah,' and the next thing I know he's coming at me with a board, an actual board, a two-by-four. I grabbed it and he's probably still lying there."

"You hit him with the board?"

"No, I hit him with my fist. He lost the board the

second after it swung over my head because, instead of swinging short, he swung long, and I went in and beat the crap out of him. I creamed him. That gives me a sense of power."

This case had an unexpected ending. Donald's father died suddenly of a heart attack and a remarkable transformation occurred in the boy. Within two months he was attending evening classes to complete his education, he had lost weight, and he had stopped drinking. He had found where he "fit" and, no longer afraid of success, he was pursuing it in a positive way.

The transition from adolescence to adulthood is not abrupt and definite, but takes a number of years. Through the maturation of the biological being (the chemical revolution of puberty is over) there comes a gradual consolidation of the personality traits. New tasks, new horizons, new challenges open up. Independence from the primary family is occurring. The wish to build a better society is now blended and somewhat mitigated by a better appraisal of what *is* from what should be. Yet this is a time when some people meet with unexpected difficulties. As a young adult meets responsibilities that go beyond the familiar—namely, family and school—success is not immediately rewarded. You don't get an A in your work as you do in an exam. The need for recognition partly determined by the habit of the school years is very strong. And when it is not forthcoming, the individual has trouble measuring success—success now is less visible because it is estimated differently. And therefore the fear of success at this stage is, in turn, further camouflaged. This is one of the major reasons that the fear of success in adults is rarely spontaneously seen by them. But it is there and it can be modified, as I will now show.

Part III

Adult Patterns of the Fear of Success

7

THE PETER PRINCIPLE IN REVERSE

In the adult, the fear of success can manifest itself in as many ways as there are personality characteristics and quirks—that is to say, in an almost unlimited fashion. However, in my work as a therapist I have noted that there are several patterns for the fear of success that repeat themselves frequently enough to be considered guidelines. In the pages that follow I will describe some of the cases that fall into the major categories of adult fears of success. They show in the most graphic terms what this fear can do to our lives and how the problem is approached by the psychiatrist and the patient. Obviously, these are not complete cases by any means. I offer them only as an indication of how adults can be helped first to recognize and then to confront their situation, which is an important step toward the resolution of the fear of success, and which the reader should view in this regard.

For ease of classification, I have grouped the first category of cases under a blanket term—The Peter Principle in Reverse. The Peter Principle, as articulated by Laurence J. Peter in his book of that name, states that "in a hierarchy every employee tends to rise to his level of incompetence." An employee may start out in a position of competence—a job that he can handle satisfactorily—but inevitably he gets promoted to a position where he is incompetent. The following examples illustrate the Peter Principle in Reverse. I propose that when the fear of success is present in persons who are qualified achievers, these persons will be promoted to the level of their competence—except that their fear of success hampers their perception so that they believe the level of their competence is actually the level of their incompetence. In each case, therapy ultimately helped the person to regard his current success as a positive factor in his life, legitimate and earned, and prepared him to accept favorably and without anxiety the possibility, indeed the inevitablity, of his next achievement. This was accomplished by taking an inventory of the individual's assets and talents in more than one area.

Mr. R., a research physicist came to see me suffering from depression. As he described it, his was a continuous kind of depression that followed each of his accomplishments. I then learned that Mr. R. got his Ph.D. from Caltech at the age of twenty-nine, and that he moved rapidly to the top of his profession. He worked extremely hard and neglected his social life in his drive to become successful, but he had always done that since early childhood. By the time he reached forty, however, Mr. R. was becoming aware that he led a lopsided existence. He was conscious that his success did not help him to enjoy life, and he was also disturbed about something else.

"Every time I get a new thought, every time a hypothesis presents itself, I get scared and depressed," he told me. "I don't understand this at all. I expect to be happy, but instead, I feel anxious, for reasons that escape me. Sure, there's some pleasure mixed in, but that fear bothers me—it's inappropriate. If it had happened only once, I would disregard it, but it happens all the time. In fact, every time I come close to a scientific discovery, I feel it strongly."

"Did you experience it in childhood as well?" I asked him.

"Let's see." He made an effort to remember. "Oh yes, in grade school every time I knew the answer in math class before anyone else, the other kids resented it. I was almost tempted to pretend I didn't know, but my mother was very ambitious for me and she encouraged me to show my abilities. The fear I felt in math class, though, is like the one I experience now."

"And how was your social life in your early years?" I inquired.

"Zero," he said flatly. "I hardly did anything except my homework and I read. That was all I cared about. I never had a date until I met my future wife, when she was visiting my cousin. She seduced me and I married her—or rather, she married me and, as you know, it didn't last. She wanted children and I refused to have them. I think the world is populated enough as it is. She also liked to go out all the time, but I had my work to do. So she left me and now I'm a bit lonely."

"How did she make you marry her?"

"She was full of smiles and never left me alone. She wanted to visit my lab and practically invited herself to come. She arranged our dates by telling me she thought it would be nice to see a certain movie or concert. She'd get the tickets and make all the arrangements. And I liked it—it made my life easier. But after we were married, she began to ask me to 'take some initiative,' as she used to say. That was easier said than done, though. I'm not a person who likes to go out; I can do very well without all that hassle. She began to get bitter about my reclusiveness and she told me she needed more of a social life. I asked her if she married me to go out or stay in, and without any hesitation she said, 'To go out.' "

"What happens if you go to a dinner party?" I asked him.

"I get nervous. My hands perspire and my stomach jumps. I run to the phone and the john, alternately. I try to seclude myself to feel better, but it's still agony." At the memory, he picked up a tissue from the box on my table and wiped his forehead with it, reliving the agonizing moments.

"Any other memories?"

"Yes. In college, after every successful exam I was depressed, but I was ashamed to admit it and, instead, I pretended to be happy. Everybody envied my success, yet I regularly got depressed after every victory, after every A, crazy as it sounds. To this day I can't figure it out. It's a mystery to me."

"What thoughts crossed your mind at the time of these depressions?"

"My thoughts were always the same. I still have them now, especially after I do something well. They boil down to two pessimistic questions: 'What's next?' and 'So what?' I always think about death as soon as I succeed in anything. After exams, even though I was usually very successful, I would start to brood and think about the futility of life. I'd ask myself, 'What good are all my accomplishments anyway, if death follows them?' But I never have these gloomy thoughts when I have to struggle, or if I meet some defeat. Actually, I guess, for me the whole process and enjoyment of life consists only in sweating over a problem, not in completing it successfully. It's the same thing with my social life. I don't need it. It's boring—all those empty conversations about nothing."

"Are you afraid of close relationships? Maybe it sounds paradoxical to you, but I think you are," I said.

"Well, if I'm successful with a woman who appeals to me, I also get depressed, the way I did when I got an A on an exam. It's fear, I know, but what can I do? I'm helpless about it."

Mr. R. was not so helpless as he thought. He had taken the first step toward recognizing his problem, and then, in subsequent sessions, I was able to help him see that his lack of social life as an adult continued the pattern he had established as a child when he had excluded others for his studies. During our discussions, I pointed out to him that now he had to practice the social exercise of exploring new territories in personal relationships in order, correspondingly, not to be afraid to venture in new directions in his work. Mr. R. first refused, but the stakes were too high for him to remain so inflexible. Therefore he reluctantly accepted a very gradual move toward social intercourse—an occasional dinner party, a family reunion. When he saw how well he survived, he was ready to consider his fear of death, which had always appeared after an accomplishment. Finally he learned to accept the fact that we are all mortal and that it is more fun to enjoy success than to suffer fear and depression, for successful or not, death is inevitable.

Mr. P. was a successful businessman who had recently ventured into politics for the first time and in an upset victory had been elected to Congress. He came to see me because of his anxiety about balancing this new role in his already crowded life. Both his business and his public responsibilities were now so demanding that he neglected his wife and children, and the resultant pressures made him impatient and sometimes even explosive at home.

I learned that as chairman of one of the larger corporations in the United States, Mr. P. had been resourceful, inventive, and imaginative. Earlier, at the university, he had been a brilliant student and outstanding in athletics. Thus, while he was still fairly young, Mr. P. had accomplished more than many people do in a lifetime. With his quick mind, Mr. P. had little difficulty acknowledging the concept of the fear of success. He was eager to examine it in himself and was highly motivated to make whatever changes would be necessary to improve his life. I am reproducing portions of our conversations at some length here because his case so clearly illustrates how the fear of success distorts the lives of even the most successful.

"What do you think about the fear of success?" I asked Mr. P. early in our sessions.

"I have been thinking back to when my business went public," he answered. "In that instance I wasn't consciously aware of the fear of success. For a year or more I had argued against going public in our business, but then when somebody dangled a good proposition in front of me—zap! I went. I don't remember any fear about it. I do remember, however, the agonies before the election for Congress. I remember thinking, 'Now I am going to have to perform in the public spotlight, and if I don't make it, or if I make a mistake, it's going to be visible to everybody'—and that was a terrible fear. I had a daydream, too, of a hook, like the old vaudeville hook used to get a performer off the stage when he was killing the show and wouldn't leave. I had the feeling that 'they' would get me by the neck with the hook and take me off. That dream would come to me usually in bed before I fell asleep, and it was frighteningly real. When it happened, I had a feeling of strangulation."

"What helped you to go on? You could have quit."

"Well, at that point I was publicly committed, and quitting seemed worse. But there were times when I did come close to quitting. Like the night I had to appear before a meeting of the League of Women Voters. Now that was a night when I almost got into the car at the office and instead of going to the meeting, I almost drove past the house and up to our place in Vermont. It was that close. I was terrified of getting up and speaking in front of all those people. It was the first time in the campaign that I had to speak in a large public arena. It was actually a debate between me and my opponent. We each made a statement and then answered questions from the audience."

"The fear was not of your opponent?"

"No, it was a fear of performing in public."

"Was it the fear of success or the fear of failure?"

"The fear was of performing in public, so it may not have been the fear of success. That fear goes back to when I was eleven or twelve years old and a pupil at Mrs. Ander's music school. She had a recital twice a year for the parents, and I remember the terror, the stark terror I had of playing at those recitals. My fear was so great I was in a flush of red-hot heat all over my body the entire time I was playing. I don't know where the fear came from or why I felt that way, but since then I've always had a fear, at least initially, of getting up on stage and performing."

"Consciously, it was a fear of failure. But could there also be a hidden fear of success? What would have happened if you had made a smash hit and become a great performer?"

"I don't know. I'm trying to remember what might have led up to my fear, but it's very difficult. It's a different kind of fear from the one I had lying in bed, thinking, 'My God, what if I win?' It was a different kind of sensation."

"It is important to differentiate the fear of failure and the fear of success. The fear you had in bed may represent two different fears, at least on the conscious level."

"Well, it's as though the fear of being elected exposed me to the idea that I wasn't nearly as good, as capable, as my business image appeared to people. The better I do, and the more people become convinced that I'm capable, the greater my fear is that I'm going to be exposed as not being capable. Yet when I got up on the stage, at campaign time, the reason why I don't think it's a fear of success in that situation is that after my first stage fright I handled it fantastically. If I really was afraid of succeeding, I don't think I'd have ended up having as much fun as I did, once I got the heat out of my body. It dropped away as I was talking, and it just disappeared when my opponent began. I ended up having fun."

"Maybe the ability to overcome that fear gave you a feeling of great exhilaration, a feeling of accomplishment. But I agree with you. I think there were two fears—the conscious and immediate fear of facing an audience, but then at night when you were afraid . . ."

"That was a fear of success," he interrupted eagerly.

"And that may have contributed, perhaps a little, to your fear of the public appearance."

"You know, the fear of success in that context is almost

as though every time I succeeded, the thing that has me by the neck is dragging me farther and farther out to a more exposed position. I'm inexorably being dragged up the ladder to the level of my incompetence. Like the Peter Principle."

"But you see, I'm talking about the Peter Principle in reverse. I have seen many people who were promoted to the level of their competence, but they thought it was the level of their incompetence."

"It's a fear that I'm going to be taken where I can't perform, a complete collapse will result, and I won't be able to face a major failure in the public eye. But it's never happened."

"What I'm trying to figure out is the difference between people who are afraid of success and succeed, and people who are afraid of success and fail because of it. You're an example of a person who succeeds in spite of the fear of success."

"So far, anyway. I've pretty well succeeded in spite of the fear up to now, but the very act of succeeding in the various things I've tried to do is pushing me another notch up the ladder and inevitably I'm going to fall. That's my fear."

"Do you believe that will happen?"

"Yes, there are many times when I think I do believe it, that I'm going to be pushed to a level where I can't cope with the pressure. And I think the fear of success will be a major part of that pressure. I'm afraid of being pushed into a situation where I'm going to be too spread out, won't be able to do a good job, and wind up a crushing failure."

"Because you have doubts about your own value?"

"Exactly."

"Well, that was certainly reflected, if you remember,

when I suggested that we should tape this conversation. Your first reaction was, 'It will probably be worthless,' instead of saying, 'Certainly. I have something to contribute. After all, I'm an experienced person living an interesting life.' "

"I was trying to make it easy for myself."

"What did you genuinely believe? That this would be worthless, or were you just being modest?"

"I think it was more a statement to cover me in case what I did say came out as garbage."

"So you considered that as a possibility?"

"Yes. In my case, I think that the fear of success is very definitely tied in with a self-image problem. If you do not have a strong enough self-image, unconsciously you feel that you don't deserve success. There's one thing that puzzles me in connection with this fear of success, though. What drives me up the ladder, now the political ladder, with increasing fear of exposure? Why do I keep going, pyramiding the scope and intensity?"

"Because your need to succeed is stronger than your fear. That is probably the answer. The fear of success in people who succeed is not as strong as their wish to achieve success. In people who fail, the fear is stronger than the wish to succeed. You are continuing because no matter how strong your fear may be, it is not as strong as your wish to succeed. I don't say that's the complete answer to the question. There are as many answers as there are different people.

"Now let's see what the dangers are in this situation that create your fear of success. First, if you wanted to become even more successful politically, it would complicate your marriage because your wife would be very unhappy. She would say, 'You'll always give most of yourself to your work and not to your family.' Second, it would be a big burden on your shoulders."

"There's another fear, too—that I'll be exposed as inadequate once I'm driven to my level of incompetence. That's the most emotionally potent fear."

"Do you still think the Peter Principle applies to you?"

"Well, I've handled everything that's come my way. I know I've done a good job of running my business and in politics. Yet there were crises where I've been pushed to the point where I wondered whether I was going to have a breakdown. There have been a couple of times in the last year and a half when I've felt under enough pressure so that I couldn't help but wonder if I'd crack. At the very least, there was the fear that at some point in going up the ladder I would hit a situation where I wouldn't be able to cope with that kind of pressure, and another Columbia reaction would take place. [He referred to his career as a graduate student at Columbia University, where his anxiety overwhelmed him and he never got his Ph.D.] Several times I was afraid that I would run from my problems because I couldn't handle them. I've seen enough to know that problems are solvable, but I'm not so sure that at my level of competence I have the ability to withstand pressure."

"Yet the only time you actually failed to accomplish what you set out to do was at Columbia. Later a deal might not come through, but it wasn't because you ran away."

"No, it's been almost as if I've been pushing myself to prove that it won't, and yet I'm wondering that in proving it won't I'll push myself to the point where it will. I don't know if that makes sense."

"This is a question of self-image. Do you see yourself, even if you don't do it, as a chief political operator? Is your self-image ready for that kind of a position? It's not only a question of whether you can do it, but whether you can see yourself doing it."

"When you say, 'Do I see myself?' I can see myself. It's not an impossible vision. But I also see myself living with a lot of fear in this role. The complexities, the pleasures—will I be well enough organized? I guess there are a lot of things I see in myself that lend themselves to a fear of success. I don't see myself as a really well-organized person. I have a tendency to procrastinate on things that aren't pleasant. Instead of getting my phone calls behind me by 11:00 o'clock Saturday morning, I let them eat away my whole weekend and make them at 8:00 o'clock on Sunday night. There are a lot of other things like that. As I look at what's involved in running a company like this, and also a political career, such weaknesses strike me as being potentially dangerous. It's a kind of weakness that tends to be magnified when the pressure is on; and that's what I'm constantly worried about—that I'll be exposed and get into a situation where I won't be able to hide this weakness. Yet, as you say, it's never happened."

"Perhaps the fear of success in politics is partly motivated by the fact that it could interfere further with success in your marriage and your business."

"That's definitely a part of it. I don't know if it's an overriding part, as compared with my fear that I'll be thrown into a position where I'll break down."

"Both play a role, I'm sure. The question is, how much of each?"

"If I were to end up in an even more important political position, it's very easy to see myself responding to the feeling of responsibility that would go with it by finding any number of reasons why I couldn't spend enough time at home or supervising my business. What remains is a fear that I find events dictating to me, and I lose the feeling that I'm controlling my life."

"In other words, if you accept a very high responsibility, then you're not in control, the position is in control of you."

"Exactly."

"That's still another factor in the fear of success."

"Absolutely. I'm afraid that the course of my life is being dictated to me by my work."

Eventually, Mr. P. was able to accept the challenge of a political life without feeling threatened by its control over him. He did an excellent job as a congressman for two terms but did not choose to run again or to run for a higher office. He had overcome his fear of success about that area of his life and had then decided it no longer absorbed him as it had before he conquered his anxieties about it. In this respect, Mr. P.'s case illustrates the discrepancy between fantasy and reality in an individual's life.

Mr. T. was a college senior, a brilliant student in the classroom and in sports. Having come from a family of academicians, however, his real success was based on intellectual achievement. He is a prime example of how a successful student can suffer from the fear of his own success.

"What do you think about the fear of success?" I asked Mr. T. "You tell me you live in a small city where you're famous as an outstanding student and so everybody knows you. People you've never even met know you, and yet you're unhappy about it. How do you explain that?"

"Well," Mr. T. said, "I wanted people to care very much about me. I wanted them to care about me for myself as a person, not for my intellect—to see me as a whole person."

"But your intellect, your size, your nose, the way you walk and talk—everything blends into what you are. To say, 'I want to be liked for myself, not my intellect,' is naïve and unrealistic. People like a person because of a combination of factors. So why worry about how people appreciate you? Why not accept your success on all levels? If some people respect you for your intellect, consider that an acceptable success. Don't fear it just because it isn't acceptance on every level. And in any case, what is the danger of being successful—of being famous in your own town?"

"Well," Mr. T. said, "it would be a hindrance to the kind of relationships I would like to have with people. I am known, one, for being very smart as a scholar, but also for being just the opposite—very reckless and irresponsible. I had two best friends, not just one, and to me that was not contradictory because they represented two extremes. Alex was very scholarly, but Brad was just the opposite, irresponsible and reckless."

"What are you?"

"I indulge myself very often."

"How? Give me an example."

"Okay. When a person turns sixteen in Connecticut, the first thing he does is to go down to Port Chester, New York, and get drunk. I used to get drunk on school nights."

"Well, is that a big sin?"

"It isn't such a big sin, but if you're busy with your studies all the time and you're a scholar, you don't do things like that."

"Do you feel guilty about it?"

"Not at all. I enjoyed myself."

"Do you think you should feel guilty about it?"

"No."

"Do you want to be recognized for it?"

"No, but I was."

"You mean you have the reputation of being a great drunk?"

"No, but I had the reputation of being somebody who could enjoy himself and did enjoy himself."

"And did that bother you?"

"Not at all."

"So here you are, not bothered by a success in an area where people say, 'Oh, look at Charles, he can get smashed, he can put away a six-pack like nothing.' This kind of success didn't bother you?"

"No."

"But the kind of success where people say, 'Look, he's a genius, he's so smart.' That bothers you. What's so threatening about such success? You still haven't given me an answer."

"Because irresponsibility and recklessness—they don't raise the kind of false facade that intellectual genius does, at least in my mind. In other words, if you're a reckless slob, there's not much you can make out of that."

"There's no promise, and consequently no disappointment, you mean."

"Yes, there's no disappointment and there's nothing to be pretentious about. It's not something you can frame and hang on your wall and be proud of. It's a fact, and people take it and like it, or they don't. The other isn't quite that simple."

"The other makes you self-conscious?"

"In my case it does."

"Is it because your self-image isn't so lofty as your reputation? Is it a false facade?"

"No, I don't think my reputation is undeserved. But I

do think that indulging in that kind of reputation can build up too many false facades."

"What are the dangers it could lead to? Give me an example."

"I can't speak from my own experience. I tend to draw conclusions from observing other people who have done this kind of thing. I have been very close to people who are extremely intelligent, and that was their sole source of energy. In other words, the more intelligent they became, the stronger they were, until in effect they didn't need any outside source of energy. And then, in their relationships, that's what they thrust upon other people—their intelligence—to impress them, to control them."

"Well, we all know there are phonies in this world, and people who exaggerate their virtues. Are you one of them?"

"No."

"Are you afraid you'll be corrupted by public opinion and become like them?"

"Maybe."

"Power corrupts, is that it? And if your reputation gives you power, then you may become corrupted and become a phoney? That's an unjustified fear, because people who even think about that are safe already. People who get drunk on power, or drunk on reputation, don't think about it. They don't reflect on it."

"At the university I got close to faculty people very quickly, extremely quickly, and on a very personal basis, and these people suddenly got very interested in me. But as soon as they mentioned anything about my capabilities in their department, in terms of being a student who showed promise, I panicked."

"Perhaps that's because you have doubts about yourself, in spite of your success in the intellectual world.

When you're among other intellectuals you panic, because they may take a deeper look and find something that's not so good as it looks on the surface. It's my hypothesis that you are afraid of success because it would lead to greater demands and therefore the risk of failure."

Mr. T.'s allergy to praise from his professors was a result of his doubts about himself and his misinterpretation of his professors' approach as exploitive—they would drain his knowledge—rather than supportive. In order for Mr. T. to overcome his fear of success, he first had to develop a basic trust in himself and then in the people who were helping him to succeed. We accomplished this through role-playing. He alternated the roles of student and professor until he could see for himself that helpful overtures can be genuine in themselves. And once he lifted that burden of suspicion from his shoulders, he was free to pursue his goals.

For Mr. L., a successful clergyman and teacher, the question of whether he was worthy of success drove him to see me. A vigorous, eloquent man, he seemed to emanate success and, in fact, he inspired success in many of the people who came into contact with him. But others resented him for just these traits and he recognized that, as a result, interpersonal conflicts developed with some of the people with whom he worked. As we talked, it became clear that this outspoken man, who stood firmly on the side of the underdog, apparently did not think it was necessary to be careful about his methods of dealing with people who interfered in the realization of his ideals. When I pointed out to him that he might antagonize people purposely to avoid success, he was interested in the idea that the fear of success exists and pursued it eagerly.

"I guess I've been afraid of success in almost every area where I have any talent at all. Years ago, for example, I met a pretty girl in the London underground and talked with her, but I didn't make a date."

"Do you remember the reason why?"

"As I recall, I don't think I attached a reason to it."

"What would have happened if she had said yes?"

"I probably would have found some device so that I could withdraw from the situation."

"That's the fear attached to it. Let's go a step further. A fear is usually triggered by danger, so suppose she'd said yes, and you then struck up a friendship with her. What would have been the ultimate danger?"

"Success."

"But what kind of success would be dangerous? And why would it be dangerous?"

"I don't think I ever established that."

"Do you think the girl would have been disappointed in you if she had known you well?"

"That turns out to be the problem, of course, with other people and other situations. It's a very common denominator in my withdrawing from social relationships."

"So, then, because of some doubts you have about yourself, you think success will lead to failure when someone finds out what you really are. That relates to the girl in London. Can you think of any other examples in your life?"

"When I was twenty-four, after I got out of the service, I hitchhiked to California to attend a national conference of young people from my church, which was my father's church. After I'd made two or three speeches at the conference, I was elected president. At the time I didn't realize the degree to which I could carry a group of people just through my preaching ability. I still don't quite understand it, but it works."

"It never occurred to you that you might be talented?"

"I keep on getting proof of it. Last week the rector put a notice in the bulletin that I was going to help him with pastoral calling while he was away on a vacation, and the phone has been ringing all week with calls from everywhere in the parish. I'm having a wonderful time, but the thing that is really a cause for anxiety is that no matter how careful I am, the people of the parish are going to push me up the ladder. They're going to insure a degree of success for me that will be a terrible threat to the rector, and he's in a position to react badly."

"Therefore, success is dangerous for you again?"

"Terribly dangerous in this instance."

"But how do you know that your work won't carry enough momentum and have enough strength so that he'll be powerless to defeat you because your success will be so strong?"

"Simply because I think that at this juncture in his life, he's perfectly capable of making a deathbed effort to prevent me from making any inroads on his power."

"Then he's afraid of your success? Because he would rather have a much less impressive person around him so he can be boss?"

"I'm not sure that's his motive, although it may be part of it. I think he honestly feels I'm not the right man at the right time, and that I'll carry a large group of people with me and create a big division in the parish. Anyway, outside of the church, lots of good things are happening now. School has improved considerably. And the most wonderful and strangest thing of all is that my blood pressure is back down to where it was when I was in high school."

"That *is* wonderful. One of the successes of psychotherapy is that blood pressure does go down, and that's a success you don't have to be afraid of. Creative people such as artists, authors, sculptors, and musicians are afraid that the success of therapy will decrease their ability to continue as creative artists."

"They see the creativity squeezed out."

"Yes, but it's exactly the opposite. As their inhibitions and conflicts become less intense, their creative ability soars."

"Well, the problem in my professional orientation is something different. I could have been rector of a very large parish, where I would have had the resources to do the kind of thing I know I could do well, but I've always done something to prevent this, even to the point right now of being head of the English department in my school. I'm constantly telling people that my work in the ministry is really a hobby, that I'm having fun while everyone else is working. I've actually said this to people, and it's a ploy. I go into a parish with this attitude and apparently I can bring enormous numbers of people along to the point where their own enthusiasm and support is just overwhelming—and it overwhelms me. I begin to withdraw and to do things calculated to turn it the other way."

"What is the danger here? That once you become top dog, people will recognize your weakness, your hollowness?"

"Yes, exactly."

Later, Mr. L. wrote me a remarkable letter analyzing his fear of success: "At the moment," he wrote, "I feel successful, and I feel a genuine and at times intense desire for more success. It's a new feeling and has remained at the forefront of my emotions and my thoughts for several weeks. I do not doubt its reality or its permanence.

"For years I have had no trouble in achieving anything

I wanted, and so many things have simply come my way that it was only necessary to say 'yes' to numbers of them to be successful. I have never been turned down for any job I ever craved, and have on the contrary turned down two calls from large parishes and a number of overtures from others.

"And yet always there has been a feeling of unworthiness. Or I have come to the point where my fears and anxieties were so great that the job, successful as it was and could have continued to be, threatened me, and it seemed easier and safer and (so I convinced myself) more exciting to go on to new tasks in new places. I often sensed this response as running away, but never, of course, understood its cause. Or never faced it. And then there is my problem with colleagues.

"Years ago a teacher was discussing with me my disappointment at one of my groups of students and he said, 'Everything you touch turns to horseshit.' That remark has stayed with me—painfully—ever since. What is even more painful is that I could see some truth in that comment. I don't think the comment was merely malicious. Also during that very open conversation the headmaster said that he thought I was a person with little inner security. Of course, I never had seen myself that way. He apparently was sensing something else—what I believe you have called a 'poor self-image.' And I have come to believe I have it, my successes and gifts notwithstanding.

"As my wife read what is just above she remarked that I should really counterbalance all this with a detailed account of my achievements. I think it's interesting that she thought of the successes, while I have been preoccupied with the mechanisms of avoiding them.

"What I have now concluded is that while I am not

afraid of added responsibilities or challenges should I achieve success, I am afraid that my inner weaknesses will spoil the apparently strong and attractive image that people develop of me."

In this case there was a conflict within Mr. L. as to his perception of what a preacher, a teacher, and a friend should be—self-effacing, modest, unobtrusive, supportive—and what his actual personal talents were. He was self-confident, masterful, visible, assertive. I showed him the difference between appearance and substance, that as long as the superficial glitter of his image did not tarnish his wholesome values, his appearance and his ideals would not conflict. As he began to accept this distinction, he found new courage to pursue his pastoral and personal relationships in depth.

8

NOT FOR WOMEN ONLY

Women have the same fears of success that men have and some special ones of their own. In today's changing times the role of women is changing fast. Whether women will be working persons or homemakers or a combination of both at various times in their life, their role models are different now from the standard ones of the past. This cultural alteration means that the measurements women previously used to determine their success in life may not be applicable in the later decades of the twentieth century. Thus, women's fears of success are both the same as and different from their mother's generation.

Mrs. D., a successful author-professor who graduated Phi Beta Kappa from a leading university, came to me because of her tensions concerning future promotions.

"When you hear the words 'fear of success,' what kind of thoughts come to your mind?" I asked her.

"What comes to mind right away is that this is a very

realistic fear, because essentially what does success mean? It implies a certain change, by definition. Success means moving on to something new, which is defined as more desirable than the previous condition. I believe the reason we don't think about this fear as being realistic, and why people usually aren't aware even of the concept, is because of the tremendous value and emphasis our society places on success. In this country success is a religion, a highly valued concept, and it's almost sinful to suggest that success might not be good. But in the name of success and for success, many things are done that really are painful to people and that create very difficult situations—situations of adjustment and change, of breaking away from relationships, giving up friendships, and moving away from rewarding situations.

"For example, an executive hardly can refuse a promotion even if it involved moving with his family to a place that might be most uninteresting. If he refused it, he'd consider himself a failure. Such a refusal rarely would be seen as a sign of something positive.

"I think we glorify and worship success. It's something that's extremely elusive. If you feel good about yourself, no matter where you are in the pecking order, then you're successful. But we usually see success in terms of occupational social climbing, changes and improvement, and that can be a painful experience, requiring a great deal of readjustment. So I think the fear of success is very realistic. We tend to repress it, and we rarely allow it to come to the surface, and if it does come, we try to ignore it or suppress it. It's not something we're proud of. People are supposed to be successful, to strive for success."

"As a woman are you afraid of success because it might put you in competition with men?"

"I think it's much more complicated," Mrs. D. said, "because there is also the fear of success for its own sake. It's a double fear of success, the same fear that men have, combined with the fear of competition with men. But an emancipated woman who's satisfied with the role of a single person and has no intention of getting married probably would have only the same kind of fear of success that a man has. But a woman who's married, or wants to be involved in a meaningful relationship with a man, probably sexually, would find the situation more complicated. Not only would she have the double fear I mentioned, but she might threaten him somehow, and then have to retreat. Very few men can take a successful woman. Basically, I think most men are chauvinistic, even the ones who pay lip service to Women's Lib."

"When did you first experience a fear of success?"

"The first time I was asked to teach at an Ivy League college. I was relatively young then, and a few days before I was supposed to start teaching, I had tremendous fears. I was so upset and nervous that I was about to call the chairman of the department and tell him I wasn't going to do it. I was afraid to take on the responsibility of teaching, although from an occupational standpoint, it was a tremendous jump up for me. I knew it was an honor to be asked, and that it implied a great amount of prestige—definitely an improved position. Yet I was simply petrified by the responsibility and I would have called the chairman and backed out if my husband hadn't prevented me.

"Earlier, when I had any major examinations, I was afraid to face them even though I knew I would do well. These were very real fears. At that point I couldn't call them by name as a fear of success, but I certainly was frightened by them. Now I understand them."

"Why did you fear success?"

"Because it implied a new situation, a readjustment, making a greater effort than the one I'd made before. By definition, it implied a more important and consequently a more difficult position—more difficult than something I'd had previously, otherwise it wouldn't be considered success. So I feared the added responsibility, and feared that maybe I wouldn't be able to do it, mixing, in my own head, the fear of success with the fear of failure.

"At every point in my career, when I moved ahead I always felt that somehow 'they' would find out I wasn't so good as I appeared to be, as others thought I was, and if I moved to a better, more successful position, 'they' would eventually find out that I didn't belong there. Then I'd be a failure and not live up to the expectations of those who had given me the position."

"How do you differentiate between the two—the fear of failure and the fear of success?"

"For me, it's very difficult to differentiate. It's much easier for an outside observer. An outsider looking at me would consider me fit, and he would define my fear as the fear of success. But somebody else might say, 'She's not good enough to reach this position and her fear is justified. She's afraid to fail.' That's why I have a hard time differentiating. Maybe in my case it's harder because the two fears are so intermixed. Generally I think that people who don't believe in themselves strongly, and yet are put in positions where they are successful and move ahead from one place to another have a much harder time differentiating between what is fear of success and what is fear of failure.

"That's really my case. For years I didn't believe in myself and I still don't in many areas. So for me, the two fears are intertwined. If I could somehow be convinced that I was going to be excellent in my next position, I wouldn't be afraid. But I'm convinced I won't do well in a new job, that I won't belong, that I won't be good enough, and so I want to run, because I'm afraid to be a failure."

"Are there areas where you don't experience the fear of success?"

"Oh, yes. In relation to my children I'm not afraid of success. And in relation to my friends I think I'm a very good friend and I relish my success. My friends appreciate me and I appreciate them. I may not make friends easily, but once I make them, I hold them. I'm not afraid to move ahead with a friend and develop the relationship into something deeper. So, obviously, there are certain areas where I'm confident, and there the fear of success doesn't enter."

"Probably there are moments in your life when you experienced the fear of success more intensely."

"I think that where the jump ahead was a major step, then the fear was much greater. But when it was a very gradual step, I hardly felt it. I also think that if the position is specified, if you know what's expected, and the movement upward is gradual and smooth, with society specifying the different steps, then the fear is much less intense. A good example is being first an undergraduate in college, where you do very well, then later you're a graduate student and also do well, and finally you're a Ph.D. and expected to take on a teaching position.

"In my case, though, it was a sudden jump after I passed my orals. I was still a graduate student when I was asked to teach, and that was a very unusual thing. I had never taught before, and suddenly I was asked to join one of the leading university faculties in the country, and I didn't have my Ph.D. yet. I knew the position was very important, and that many Ph.D.'s would be happy to teach there, but they hadn't been asked, and I had. It was so unexpected and unusual that it meant a tremendous jump for me at that particular point. I worry about still another giant career step. One always wants it, but that's when the fear is strongest."

Here the fear of failure and the fear of success were blended perfectly. Thus the emphasis in therapy was to help Mrs. D. recognize that she had already taken a "giant career step"—her first professional teaching assignment—and had found, in retrospect, that she had been competent. When she focused on that earlier fear and on its subsequent resolution, she developed the necessary insight to face future opportunities without the previous accompanying anxiety. She now knew that, having once overcome her fear of success, she could certainly do it again.

Ms. G. came to me because, as an achiever who wanted to play as well as to work, she felt guilty. Her father was an alcoholic and her mother was a self-effacing, mild-mannered woman. Her three brothers had spotty records in school and appeared to lack direction. Ms. G. was the success in the family. In high school, Ms. G. had a short, psychotic breakdown, but that condition soon subsided and did not occur again. When she came to me she was a senior in college and limped into the office with her leg in a cast, recently having had knee surgery. I asked her how she felt.

"Well," Ms. G. said, "I'm afraid of physically recovering from my knee injury. It's related to my views of my work, I know. I'm afraid of having my knee remain bad, and I'm afraid of failing, of my work going badly. At the same time, I'm afraid of having to cope with new situations when my knee is well and when I'm successful with my work."

"You think that a combined recovery will just lead to greater challenges?"

"It certainly would lead to more challenges, and to more confrontations with people, because I'd consider myself whole again and there wouldn't be any deterrent to my work or my relationships. I know I'm going to have more relationships with people than I had when I was sick both times, and I do want to be involved again, but I've had so many bad involvements in the past I'm afraid there will be more failures. But if these relationships do succeed, I don't know where they might lead."

"What would be the danger? What could they lead to?"

"Well, I don't know how to handle long-term relationships. For example, I can't imagine myself getting married—now that's a fear."

"Are you afraid of the physical aspect of marraige?"

"No, not the physical. I don't know about the emotional part. It's just that I can't see myself involved in a relationship that would endure. Yet I have to admit I'm just as much afraid of not being involved, of becoming all wrapped up in my work."

"Success in work, then, could lead you away from success with men?"

"Yes, it might, but just as I'm afraid of failure in not being involved, I'm also afraid of a failure if my work is lost in a marriage or in some other relationship. But then, I'm just as afraid of succeeding in my work because I don't know where it will lead me. I really don't know what I can do with it, because I don't know the field that well. I don't know where I can go as a person, or as a woman, because there are a lot of authority challenges involved."

"Are you considered a successful person by your peers?"

"In my work, yes."

"Do you consider yourself successful in your work?"

"Yes, and I know I'm well thought of by both my family members and my peers. They give me plenty of support and assurance."

"Let's suppose you continue to succeed in your work. Then the only danger you see is that success with it may take you away from other successes, like a family life."

"Well, I think work can become a substitute, and that's what it has been for me in the past year and a half—a substitute for relationships. I've put all my energies into my work, and now I'm starting to diffuse them. I don't want my work to suffer, but I'm willing to subtract from it, because, as a person, I need to succeed not just in my work but in my relationships, and in terms of the interests I have outside of work. I need to feel more rounded."

"Let's pretend, then, that you've accomplished every possible success professionally. You've reached the peak you desire. What would it be? What is that peak?"

"It would be that I had graduated from college, from graduate school, and that I was in a firm doing design work that I thought satisfied some need and had some value."

"Okay. Now let's pretend for a moment that you've already accomplished this. It's quite possible, you know. Is there any danger in accomplishing it?"

"Yes, because the demands on your time are so great in that field, your family or other relationships can suffer.

So it might mean success in reaching those goals, but your personal life would suffer."

"It may be too much, then?"

"I don't think it has to be too much. I believe you ought to be able to go home from your work and put it aside."

"But the fear exists nevertheless?"

"Yes, because I've always neglected myself and other people for my work. But I now feel a much stronger urge, a need to do other things besides my work. I've started to play the flute again. I'm more interested, in fact, in just living again—doing busy work like needlepoint and other things that take me away from my work. And doing them not because they're another outlet or a place to hide, but because they contribute to me as a person. You just can't survive on your work alone and succeed, because then you're lacking other sources of information, other people's ideas, other people's viewpoints. So you have to succeed not only with your work but as a person, with other people.

"But it's almost like a fight to keep myself balanced, to go on working and to keep myself from being afraid of succeeding. At the beginning of this term I was so afraid of really doing well that I put my work off and just played, to an extreme extent. I stayed away from my work, and then I saw that I was afraid of doing well, of having the faculty accept me not just as a woman but as a person. It took me about four weeks to dig in, and then I tried harder."

"Looking back, did you have a fear of success as a child? Can you trace your fears to some early experiences?"

"When I was a child there was never any suggestion that I would have a profession. I was brought up in a family where girls weren't thought of as working. And that's been the major concern and problem in my studying to be a professional."

"How old were you when you first realized that not working was a sort of built-in family tradition?"

"I think I was fifteen or sixteen. I still didn't have any idea of what I wanted to do, but I knew that in my own family and the families my mother associated with, none of the women were professionals. They wouldn't have considered working and marrying, or working and not marrying."

"Were you a good student when you were ten years old?"

"I was a good student in the sixth grade."

"First grade?"

"I don't remember."

"But you remember the sixth grade. Were there any feelings connected with being a good student that made you uneasy in any way?"

"I was a social outcast. By the time I got to the sixth grade, I was at the top of my class, and I was a straight-A student right through junior high, but that seemed to mean that I was excluded from any social life. Kids my age at that time were dating. I wasn't considered as a date because they said I was always reading, and everybody thought it was strange for a girl to read and not flirt with the boys. But I wasn't interested in boys at that time or in dating. In the sixth grade I had only two friends, and they were both bright girls."

"Did you say to yourself, 'I'd be better off if I weren't such a good student'?"

"Well, I didn't think I'd be better off. I wanted both, and it bothered me tremendously until I was fifteen or sixteen, when I had to go see a doctor because I couldn't balance things for myself anymore. I couldn't stand not to have both."

"Do you think there's a way to do both?"

"I know there is now, but I couldn't find it when I was that age."

"So it's easier at twenty-one?"

"It's still hard, very hard."

"Do you know anyone who actually could do it?"

"I think I could do it. But it takes a long time, a lot of thought, and a lot more planning to be able to do your work and be involved with other people at the same time."

"Now, another question. Do you think that talking about the fear of success, as we're talking now, will be useful to you in identifying it as an entity, so that you can deal with it better?"

"Yes, I do. I've talked with a friend at school, a woman who's a very strong feminist. And I've talked with a boy I met while I was in the hospital. They've made it easier for me to see my own fears and to recognize them when I start pulling back in a relationship or pulling back from my work. I know you can't let the issue drop. I mean it's always going to be there, because there's such a balance between the fear of success and the fear of failure."

"They're together?"

"Yes, you can't separate them."

"But it's good to identify them."

"Yes, good to identify them, know them, and acknowledge them, not just talk about them. You have to acknowledge these fears within yourself. I think I missed acknowledging this fear because I never thought of success for myself as a person until I was at that really crucial age, about fifteen or sixteen. That's when I started thinking about it. But no one talked about it because no one I knew would consider talking to a woman about success in terms of her life. It's as though success were hidden in the closet."

With Ms. G., the fear had come out of the closet. She could now recognize it, talk about it, and begin to understand it. Every time a fear is confronted, as Ms. G. confronted the fear of success, it has a good chance to be resolved, because recognition neutralizes the anxiety of the unknown, and that anxiety of the unknown is what is experienced as fear. As a result of her new self-knowledge, Ms. G. has found a place in her life for both play and work, and now is able to balance her emotional and professional life to her satisfaction.

Ms. A., a woman in her thirties, was an only daughter who lived in the shadow of her father, from whom she had inherited an auto-parts manufacturing business. Her father had never ventured into his manufacturing plant during his lifetime and had kept himself locked in his office in a different part of town. He refused to have any contact with his workers, although, like most of them, he had never graduated from college. After his death, Ms. A. found herself continuing in the same pattern.

I asked her why she wasn't going to the plant she now owned.

"The reason is simple," she said. "It's a two-hour plane flight from where I now live. It doesn't make sense for me to go there."

"When were you there last?" I asked.

She seemed not to hear my question. "I get a good income from it anyway, so why should I be greedy?" she said.

I repeated the question a little differently: "When were you last in your hometown?"

"What? I didn't hear you." I could see she sincerely

believed that she hadn't heard what I said. People often don't realize they have heard something. Their resistance interferes.

"You heard me," I said.

"No, I didn't," she protested.

"Try to guess what I said."

"Why should I?"

"Consider it an experiment."

"But I didn't hear you."

"Try anyway. If you knew what I said, there wouldn't be any need for guessing. Guessing is only useful when we don't know."

"When did I go to the plant last—was that it?"

"Exactly. You see, when you allowed yourself the freedom of uninhibited guessing, when you weren't afraid to make a mistake, your guess was right. Remember, there's no penalty for guessing."

"Do you guess often?"

"All the time. Actually, a good diagnostician is a doctor who can guess the right illness on the basis of very few facts. When everything is known, a correct diagnosis is obvious, but the real skill is to be able to do it with a minimum of information and be right."

"So you want me to practice guessing?" Ms. A. asked.

"Yes, because it will help you to overcome your fear of success."

"What are you talking about?"

"Let me explain. Your father was afraid of success in his factory because, as you told me earlier, his aspirations were academic, not toward business. He never went to college, yet because of his wealth, he was a member of an exclusive country club, where he was the only one without a higher education."

"But he made money in the plant without going to college."

"Yes, but he believed he would have made much more if he had, and besides, he was living with the incredible inhibition of being afraid to trespass on his own property."

"He was afraid to mix with the people at the plant," she said. "What you're saying is that he deprived himself of the pleasure of a successful businessman who oversees every part of his enterprise."

"Yes, and he was keeping up the illusion of a man who is really an academician or a superfinancier. Mixing with the workers at the plant would threaten that image."

"It's true. I know he was ill at ease with the workers, and with the club members, too. He never knew how to relax and never enjoyed my company, even though I was his only child."

"So now you understand that there is no need to imitate your father. You can look after your own business."

It wasn't so easy as that, of course. Ms. A. was reluctant at first, but a month later she made a trip to the plant and talked with the manager. Within the following year she was able to make several visits, each one more efficient than the last. She stopped being an absentee owner and she established a relationship with the workers. The satisfaction she derived from participating in her own business was not only emotionally gratifying, but increased her income. Now that she no longer identified with her father's fear of success, she enjoyed her new life. Before her therapy, fear of success in business meant doing better than her father, and that simply was not acceptable.

Mrs. W., a fine opera singer, knew success from childhood. She came from a modest American home, but her talent brought her quickly into contact with the musical élite of the world. She had a disastrous first marriage to a man who valued her career more than he did her. She has had an up-and-down relationship with her present husband, who prefers to sacrifice her voice for the sake of their marriage.

At one point in her therapy she said: "I've always had this fear of being dominated by my voice."

"But how can you be dominated by your voice?" I asked.

"For instance," Mrs. W. answered, "I wanted very much when I was growing up to be a philosopher, to read. I was an avid reader, and at eleven or twelve I was reading by myself constantly. By the time I was seventeen, I was extremely interested in Zen Buddhism, and a lot of other things that had to do with religions and mysticism. Anything that had to do with the mind fascinated me tremendously. My mother was very worried about that, and she didn't like it any better when I went to art school and began to draw and paint. She was against any activity that detracted from my voice. I was also very popular with the boys and very conscious of them. I think I got married as young as I did in order to get out of the house, away from my mother. It didn't work, though. She came to visit me every day, and I could see that she lived through me, particularly through my singing. My husband did the same thing.

"My relationship with my first husband wasn't as satisfactory as my second. In the first place, my present husband and I have a marvelous relationship, whether it's physical, spiritual, or intellectual. It's a very flowing, very active relationship. With my first husband it wasn't active because, if he knew I had to sing somewhere, he would be extremely careful. If he had a cold, he wouldn't even kiss me. He was like my mother; everything had to be subordinated to my singing."

"Do you think he preferred your singing to you, then?"

"Yes, he did."

"Now I understand the fear of success about your voice," I told her. "If your voice is appreciated more than you are, you're the loser through your success. But would you consider making an alliance with your voice instead of continuing the rivalry?"

"Well, I'm certainly splintered between myself and my voice, and the result is that every time I've been close to real success I've blown it."

"Tell me what you have done to blow it. Earlier you mentioned gaining weight, and I think you also told me you don't sing well after you're highly praised."

"That's right. If I had a performance, I'd always see to it that I was worried about something, worrying about even one passage, and worrying so much I would actually destroy the performance and the opportunity. You know, if you handle anything too much, you destroy it."

"You remarked before about something that happened with Stravinsky. What was that?"

"I was a very young student at the time his opera, *The Rake's Progress,* was done at the Met. He didn't like the performance, so he decided to conduct it himself at the Boston University Conservatory, the only time he ever did that. I auditioned for him, and it was like the first time I sang. There was no applause when I finished and I was so afraid that I started to walk back to the dressing room. Then they started, and they applauded for a half hour and never stopped, and then I was really afraid. Mr. Stravinsky told me he had never heard his music sung so well, and went on praising and praising me, and I just couldn't go on."

"So your singing after Stravinsky's praise wasn't so good as it could have been?"

"Oh, no. At the Stravinsky audition I was only able to get through the next aria with great pain. He chose me for the part anyway."

"You were crushed by this success?"

"Yes, and it happens that way every time."

"Crushed instead of being uplifted by it."

"That's right. Why can't I love the applause?"

It was clear that Mrs. W. would never fully realize her great talent or reconcile it with the demands of her marriage unless she could overcome her fear of success. What Mrs. W. needed to learn was that it was possible for her to be both an accomplished singer and a whole person, including a successful wife. To help Mrs. W., it was immediately apparent that we needed the cooperation of her businessman husband. We then began cojoint therapy. The strength of cojoint therapy is that the two marriage partners learn to speak frankly and subsequently create an alliance that will respect their individual needs as well as the needs of their union. Mr. and Mrs. W. each learned that they needed their independent careers and that their time together as a couple, while curtailed by their professional schedules, is adequate for their happiness as long as they let it work for them in a positive way. I helped Mr. and Mrs. W. realize that they benefited from each other's success and that that success, as a result, should be appreciated, not feared either by the individual or by the marriage.

Part IV:

Do You Have the Fear of Success?

9

A TEST AND SOME ANSWERS

Now that we know what the fear of success means, how it develops, and what some of its more obvious manifestations are, it is time to ask—*Do you have the fear of success?* So many of us do without explicitly recognizing it, that I have drawn up a short diagnostic test. Before you ask yourself the questions on it, remember that the test requires the individual to look honestly within himself to try to measure his own fear. Every reader of this book, if he wants to help himself, must assume that he shares to a degree in the universal fear of success. He must search his mind and emotions to pinpoint the manifestations of the fear of success that may be impeding his life. That can be done by examining closely the most important areas of life—first the family and the roles and relationships of father, husband, wife, mother, brother, and sister; then business life and the relationship with peers, subordinates, and superiors; and finally, social life and the place of friends.

If this seems like a hard thing to do, consider the

consequences of never doing it. Would anybody really want to be like Jordan, whose mother says, "Wake up. Wake up. It's time to go to school."

"I don't want to go to school; I hate school," Jordan says, clinging more tightly to the bed.

"But you have to go to school," his mother insists. "Now get up. It's late."

"I hate school and I'm not going," Jordan says.

"There are two good reasons why you should go to school," his mother says. "One is that you're forty-two years old, and the second reason is that you're the principal."

That anecdote carries the fear of success to the absurd extreme, I know, but a great many people are stranded somewhere along Jordan's path. Of course, the concept of success differs for different people, depending on many variables, as we have discussed previously. The concept of success also changes depending on the time of the individual's life, and the culture and period in which he is living. In Herman Hesse's novel *Siddhartha,* three stages in the pursuit of success are described. The first, coming in adolescence, comprises a successful separation from parents and survival in the wilderness. The second is pursuit of financial and business accomplishments. Finally, at age forty, the pursuit of success is reduced to the simplicity of sitting on a riverbank and listening to the music of the water.

One person's success, of course, may be met with disregard and contempt by someone else. A wish to succeed in an army career may look ridiculous to a young man who considers the army an unnecessary evil. Similarly, success in writing may be regarded as a failing by a professional man who has no understanding of any form of reference other than his own.

As well, the wish to succeed does not limit itself to the

area of an individual's expertise. A doctor may be extremely successful in his practice, but at the same time he may seek success in business, politics, or literature. He may have little fear of success in his field, but a great deal of fear when it comes to something outside it. That is not only because he is on unfamiliar territory, but also because his new accomplishment may generate unconscious guilt since it takes him away from his main pursuit. Or the opposite situation can be true. I knew a physician who had an intense fear of success in his specialty. He went through agonies when patients showed him their gratitude after he performed successful surgery. Yet when by coincidence he branched out into a business venture, he felt free and exuberant. Eventually he closed out his medical practice and became a successful businessman. Manifestation of the fear of success, consequently, varies with the concept of what success means to a particular individual.

I have tried in the previous pages to show the fear of success in as broad a spectrum as the many forms it may take and to demonstrate its development from the earliest stages of life. Along the way I have raised the warning signs so that adolescents and adults may recognize the indications of their own fears of success and so that parents may recognize the appearance of the fear and know how to deal with it in their children.

Now it is time for the self-help steps that enable us to remove the fear of success and its crippling effects from our lives.

In working with people who have different degrees of the fear of success I have noticed that its intensity can be measured by numerous subtle factors. Each of them separately does not have major significance, but in a cluster the items determine the severity of the problem. Thus I have devised a test to measure the Fear of Success

	Wife/ Husband	*Son*	*Daughter*	*Mother*	*Father*	*Brother*	*Sister*	*Boss*	*Co-Workers*	*Sub-ordinates*	*Friends*
1. Anger											
2. Impatience											
3. Boastfulness											
4. Arrogance											
5. Sarcasm											
6. Pretentiousness											
7. Distrust											
8. Envy											
9. Fearfulness											
10. Competitiveness											
11. Breaking Promises											
12. Lying											
13. Dishonesty											
14. Conceit											
15. Insincerity											
16. Secretiveness											

17. Smugness
18. Forgetfulness
19. Carelessness
20. Detachment
21. Indifference
22. Inefficiency
23. Untidiness
24. Wastefulness
25. Stinginess
26. Pettiness

27. Meekness
28. Lack of Planning
29. Tardiness
30. Tiredness

quotient (FSQ) in each individual. The test lists a number of emotions you may be experiencing with significant people in your life. Ask yourself to what extent any of the listed characteristics interfere in your relationships, and rate the answers as to intensity: 3 points = high; 2 points = moderate; 1 point = mild.

When you have completed the FSQ Test, tabulate your scores and note the meaning of the numbers: a score of under 30 = mild FSQ; a score of 31–60 = moderate FSQ; and a score of 61–90 = high FSQ.

Suppose you find that you have a strong or even moderate fear of success in an area you consider important. There are a number of steps you can take to remedy that fear of success. While I have enumerated thirty items on the FSQ, there are actually, as I pointed out earlier, four main traits, each with a number of characteristics that cluster accordingly. As each trait undergoes modification, so, of course, will the attendant characteristics.

Let us begin, then, by modifying category number one—anger. Thus the behavioral modification tools that apply to the larger category of anger will also transfer to the clustering traits (impatience, boastfulness, arrogance, sarcasm, and pretentiousness). Actually you have already taken the first step to modify your fear of success in this area by recognizing that it interferes in the relationship or relationships that you consider important. Here behavioral modification could be of great assistance when you emphasize the positive and overlook the negative. For example, if your child brings home a good report card, yet you only glance at it before getting angry about his disheveled hair, you are shifting the emphasis in the relationship from positive contact to a negative one. And therefore what you have produced is negative reinforcement—anger is a double-edged sword with the sharper edge directed at the person expressing the anger. In order to shift negative reinforcement into positive reinforcement, you will have to become conscious of your priorities and eventually, through practice, come to a point where you will be able to disregard the chaotic-hair syndrome of the relationship and pay attention only to the good-report-card syndrome. With anger and its attendant items, the signal or warning to shift emotional gears is a tightening up, an emotional tenseness that may be either physical or psychological or both.

For the category of distrust, the trigger is different; it is verbal in form—a constant hostile questioning. A thirty-three-year-old woman came to see me because she didn't trust her husband. He was loving, attentive, a good provider, but he travels on business 50 percent of the time, and she feared that he had affairs. Her distrust for her husband created tension between them and also carried over to her relationship with her ten-year-old son, whom she constantly suspected of mischief. Her distrust had a history in her relationship with her mother, who made frequent promises to her and who invariably broke those promises. The first step in her therapy, or for anyone who suffers from a high FSQ with regard to distrust (and/or envy, fearfulness, competitiveness, breaking promises, lying, dishonesty, conceit, insincerity, secretiveness), is to note how destructive the pattern is. When this woman recognized that as soon as she saw her husband or her son she became the distrustful inquisitor and they became alienated, she realized her behavior robbed her family of affection and fun and substituted emotional blowups—no substitute indeed. Then she learned to curb her desire to ask threatening questions of her husband and son.

Smugness heads the third category (a constellation

that also includes forgetfulness, carelessness, detachment, indifference, inefficiency, untidiness, wastefulness, stinginess, and pettiness). A young dentist I knew developed a manner with patients, nurses and his family that was supercilious enough so that, despite his evident technical success, he was failing in his personal relationships. He literally walked around emotionally hidden behind a distant half-smile. The trigger or warning signal here is the eventual and unmistakable sense that "everyone is avoiding me." That shock was sufficient to motivate the dentist to confront his asocial behavior and to be more conscious of and responsive to other people.

An inventive engineer I know exemplifies the fourth personality constellation, meekness (but also including lack of planning, tardiness, and tiredness). This man was a genius at developing electrical devices, but surprisingly anxious in his relations with his wife, children, and business associates. He was unable to mobilize the energy to allow himself to stand up to demands he did not consider justified. Gradually he lost ground both at home and then at work, until a bankruptcy in both areas of his life acted as a propellant for him to change.

In each case and each personality constellation, the incentive to change a dysfunctional pattern of behavior is not an automatic corollary of insight into the fear of success, but a conscious decision that a new form of behavior would be an improvement. In my work I select a specific area for the person to practice his new pattern or patterns of behavior. For example, the man who is angry must start controlling his anger with one human target—his wife, his employer, his parent—before he can successfully apply this new behavioral form on a broader human scale. In a like manner, the distrustful person must make a conscious effort to trust a single relationship—to accept it as it appears and not as he fantasizes—before the entire category of accompanying behavior can be successfully modified. With smugness at the root of an individual's fear of success, he must be taught to listen attentively to one member of his inner circle. And with meekness, the man must be shown the advantages of taking a stand with one person with whom he deals daily. Once the individual sees the positive effect of a new patterning of behavior, he invariably develops self-confidence in that area. And this self-confidence has a radiating effect that can then be extended to other relationships until the category that caused the fear of success is neutralized so that it no longer interferes in the healthy process of life.

I find this behavioral modification program usually requires three months to show results. Should you find after that reasonable period of time that your fear of success in the area of your concern and practice is in no way diminished, then it may be time to conclude that self-help is not sufficient. At this point I would suggest setting up an appointment with a psychiatrist for an evaulation.

Let me tell you about my method of work. It may give you a clearer idea, first, as to whether you should see a psychiatrist, and, second, what the therapeutic process is.

I assume that most people sitting in my office have a great many assets and some liabilities. By definition, men and women who have succeeded in any area (and almost all have) have proved they have talent, persistence, enterprise, and courage. Therefore, I'm not surprised that in the great majority of cases the person who has already succeeded in some of his pursuits is quite ready and willing to face the challenge of overcoming a handicap he has failed to notice. Once the individual is convinced he can benefit from such a procedure, the job will be done with his cooperation. Both of us will try to clarify all the aspects of his fear of success, and at the same time devise a program, a series of steps, to be taken to overcome it. This program is basically the same one that I outlined in the self-help portion of this chapter. The only difference is that the individual has the assistance of a trained professional to monitor his new assumptions of behavioral patterns.

Treatment officially begins with the narrative the patient gives me of his life—his triumphs and disappointments, his hopes and failures, his dreams and nightmares. This narrative cements the bond between the patient and the therapist. My ability to see shape when the patient doesn't, my calm when he is anxious, helps to soothe the pain by providing understanding and an interested ear. It would be naïve, of course, to assume that complete objectivity is ever possible, but an attempt has to be made. It helps me when I imagine myself in the shoes of the person who seeks my assistance. I wonder what I would have done in his situation, and I try to understand the man not only at the moment of his present concern, but to see what can be observed through the perspective of his life history. Here it is important not to think of personality as static and frozen in its shape. No matter how many facets I consider in assessing a person's character, I realize that in different settings and with different people the individual exhibits different traits of his personality.

One of the important things I emphasize in my therapy is daring to estimate probability—to guess. I remember that when I was teaching child psychiatry in medical college, I interviewed a nine-year-old boy in the presence of four medical students. Later when the boy left the room, the students were asked to describe what they had heard and seen. They protested. It was their first seminar in child psychiatry, they said, and they were not qualified to do what I had asked. I explained that it wasn't necessary to have any professional preparation or training for what I required—to see and to hear and to venture a guess.

Guessing based on probability is an extremely rewarding and useful experience. It gives the individual confirmation of courage, exemplifying the audacity, daring, and spirit of the free mind. It's easy to talk about things that are well established, but to make a calculated guess is to enter the realm of self-discovery. Thus I now introduce to my patient the question, "What makes you afraid of success?" And I encourage the person to guess at the answers for the edification of both of us. Out of the resultant discussion, we piece together the old, destructive patterns of behavior and create the new ones to serve the individual better.

In my opinion, good therapy does not thrive on clever interpretations by the psychiatrist, but on the person's effort to find his own answers. The therapist clarifies and possibly points out flaws in logic, suggesting distortions and stimulating thinking. But ready-made answers rarely serve a good purpose and often increase the resistance to good advice. The best advice comes as a revelation to the individual.

Dr. V., head of research and development in a large corporation, was confronted with the corporation president's antagonism. As long as Dr. V. feared success, he was afraid to look for another job because, if he were successful, he "might have to move."

When I understood that his position in his present

company was hopeless, I showed him how his moving might be a blessing. Finally, after lengthy delays, he had an interview with another firm that made him a job offer he subsequently accepted. What helped him take this positive action were two revelations—realization of his own worth, and the knowledge that his wife and child would not object to moving to another state. Dr. V. would never have arrived at these new views, however, unless we had spoken at length about the poor communication he had had with his family and his lack of self-knowledge.

Ultimately, then, as this case study and all the previous examples show, I strive to help my patients learn how to diminish their fear of success through relevant self-information. To achieve this, and to recapitulate, the person has to discuss with me the pattern of success-failure programmed into his life from its beginning, he has to recognize the specificity of the fear of success as it applies to him, and he has to learn how it interferes with his pursuit of happiness. When he has done this, he has come to grips with his fear of success and neutralized its destructive effect—the aim for all of us.

INDEX